INTERCESSION

The Power and Passion to Shape History

For More Information

James (Jim) W. Goll is the cofounder of **Encounters Network** (formerly Ministry to the Nations) with his wife Michal Ann. They are members of the **Harvest International Ministries** Apostolic Team and contributing writers for *Kairos* magazine and other periodicals. James and Michal Ann have four wonderful children and live in the beautiful rolling hills of Franklin, TN.

James has produced several Study Guides on subjects such as "Equipping in the Prophetic," "Blueprints for Prayer," and "Empowered for Ministry" all available through the Encounters Resource Center.

Other Books by Jim W. and Michal Ann Goll
Fire on the Altar
The Lost Art of Intercession
Kneeling on the Promises
Wasted on Jesus
Exodus Cry
Elijah's Revolution
The Coming Prophetic Revolution
Women on the Front Lines: A Call to Courage
A Call to the Secret Place
The Beginner's Guide to Hearing God
The Seer
God Encounters
Praying for Israel's Destiny

For more information contact:

Encounters Network
P. O. Box 1653
Franklin, TN 37075
Office Phone: 615-599-5552
Office Fax: 615-599-5554
For orders call: 1-877-200-1604

For more information or to sign up for their Monthly E-mail Communiques, visit their website at
www.encountersnetwork.com
or E-Mail: info@encountersnetwork.com

INTERCESSION

The Power and Passion to Shape History

Jim W. Goll

Destiny Image® Publishers, Inc.
P.O. Box 310
Shippensburg, PA 17257-0310

"Speaking to the Purposes of God for This Generation
and for the Generations to Come"

ISBN 0-7684-2184-5

For Worldwide Distribution
Printed in the U.S.A.

2 3 4 5 6 7 8 9 10 11 12 13 14 / 10 09 08 07 06 05 04

This book and all other Destiny Image, Revival Press, MercyPlace, Fresh Bread, Destiny Image Fiction, and Treasure House books are available at Christian bookstores and distributors worldwide.

For a U.S. bookstore nearest you, call **1-800-722-6774**.
For more information on foreign distributors, call **717-532-3040**.
Or reach us on the Internet:
www.destinyimage.com

DEDICATION AND ACKNOWLEDGMENT

From the bottom of my heart, I desire to dedicate this book to the person who has influenced my Christian life and ministry more than any other single individual—the internationally acclaimed Bible teacher Derek Prince. His excellent teaching and life's example of prayerfulness has immensely impacted my life. Thank you, Lord, for allowing Derek Prince's shadow to be cast upon my life.

I am also grateful to the Lord for my dear family, who support me in all I do; to our servanthood staff and team at Ministry to the Nations; to our intercessory Prayer Shield; and to all who stand with Michal Ann and me. Lastly I want to acknowledge the team called Destiny Image Publishers. Thanks for adopting me into your heart. Blessings to each and every one of you!

May this book be another encouraging tool to help the global prayer movement continue to march forth for the sake of Jesus Christ.

With a passion for intercession,
Jim (James) W. Goll

ENDORSEMENTS

Scholarly, well researched, easily understood, and reader friendly are all accurate descriptions of *Intercession*. I realize that some of those descriptions seem contradictory, but believe me, in this case they are not. You will grow in your understanding; you will be challenged in you heart (not condemned). You will know the ways of God more thoroughly, and you will be more effective in your "lifestyle" of prayer after you read this book. And pastors, you will preach from it!

This book is urgently needed because there is no more important issue facing the Church than the one Jim Goll deals with in *Intercession*—identificational confession and intercession. No issue will have greater impact on the coming harvest than this one. I urge you to delve into this excellent book and let it change your life—and then the world as together we embrace these truths.

Thank you for your contribution to the worldwide harvest!

—Pastor Dutch Sheets
Author, *Intercessory Prayer*

Jim Goll captures the heart of God and the apostolic history of the Church, then prepares us for future victory and transformation—all in this one book. Not only does *Intercession* bring us revelation personally, but it also brings key insights on how we have a responsibility to acknowledge and eradicate sin corporately and territorially. When you read this book, you will see sin's corporate magnitude and effect on the land in which you live. However, Jim builds within your belief systems the faith and authority you need to deal with the issues confronting you. I believe that this was the Lord's attempt and method of communication. *Intercession* captures the heart and Spirit of our Savior's commissioning.

May *Intercession* cause the latter-day glory recorded in the Book of Haggai to become a reality in your life. Read, release forgiveness, and watch transformation begin!

—Chuck D. Pierce
Executive Director, World Prayer Center
Vice President, Global Harvest Ministries

Using words like bullets and phrases like spears, Jim Goll writes a classic textbook on shaping history. This book is a roadmap to restoring the power and passion of intercession. How can we have neglected it so long?

—Tommy Tenney
Director, GodChasers Network
Author, GodChaser

Intercession is a crucial book for our times. God has given Jim Goll strategic new insights that will take the Body of Christ to new levels of effectiveness in advancing the Kingdom of God here on earth. I highly recommended it!

—C. Peter Wagner
Chancellor, Wagner Leadership Institute

I read this book with shouts of joy and an overwhelming sense of relief. After a long travail, a birth of great importance has taken place. We now have a readable adventure that captures the heart of what is going on in today's prayer movements, a renewed understanding of priestly mediation. This is clear, bold teaching that cuts through confusion and equips the emerging generation for ministry to the nations.

—John Dawson
Founder, International Reconciliation Coalition

John the Baptist declared that with the appearance of Christ, "the axe is laid unto the root of the trees" (Mt. 3:10a KJV). The Church's effective expression of the redeeming virtue and ministry of Christ has often been defiled, confused, and constricted by many historic "root" transgressions. Who likes to be hit with an axe? No one. But you will be spiritually cut free from inherited prejudice if you dare to read this passionate presentation with an open heart.

—Gary Bergel
President, Intercessors for America

Intercession is full of powerful insights into the many facets of pray and proclamation. It is a passionate plea for God's people to set aside religious and cultural notions and get on with our greatest work.

—Jack Taylor
Founder, Dimension Ministries

Jim Goll's *Intercession* is an intriguing, masterfully written book. He has done the Body of Christ a great service by distilling the numerous teachings on the power of intercession. This book is certain to help release the destiny of nations. It is a must read!

—Cindy Jacobs
Cofounder, Generals of Intercession

Jim Goll's newest book, *Intercession,* is part of the growing corpus of writings that shows the way to revival. The book is timely because, if the words being spoken concerning revival will come to pass, the lessons of this book certainly must first be applied.

—Dan Juster
Director, Tikkon Ministries

This is a richly anointed book that clearly and beautifully expresses the Father's heart. It calls us to let go of our self-centered focus on attaining the glorious promises of God and to obediently lay down our lives, giving ourselves wholly to follow Him and the line of His priorities, which lead to an eventual glory that covers the earth and affects all people. With accurate scholarship in the historical review, this is a book that specifically convicts, challenges, and encourages the Church at the same time. It is a "must" for this generation!

—John and Paula Sandford
Cofounders of Elijah House, Inc.

Blending together biblical teaching, responsible research, and passion for prayer, Jim W. Goll has made a significant contribution in his latest book, *Intercession*. Blockades to revival are identified and the way to remove them is powerfully explained in practical steps. Intercessors committed to revival will benefit by reading this book.

—Mike Bickle
Director, International House of Prayer

Jim Goll listens to the Lord. He listens when he reads the Scripture. He receives fresh insights and is able to pass them along. If we will listen to what the Lord is saying through Jim and then participate, we will experience a greater outpouring of the Lord's grace and fullness for our time.

—Don Finto
Director, Caleb Company

CONTENTS

Section One

GET READY!
OUR INTERCESSORY FOCUS

Chapter 1

HISTORY BELONGS
TO THE INTERCESSORS!

◆

I want to be a history maker! That is the goal of my life. In fact, I want you to arise to your priestly and prophetic destiny and help me and thousands of others shape history before the throne of Almighty God! Are you ready to make a difference? The recipe for enduring change is simple. It is spelled I-n-t-e-r-c-e-s-s-i-o-n. Yes, prayer changes things!

Enough with this passive, neutered brand of Christianity that has invaded the Body of Christ! Let's arise and get on with God's original program of extending the rod of His Kingdom authority into every sphere of life. Let's shake ourselves free from the influences of this lethargic "what will be will be" pervasive attitude and take our rightful position—seated with Christ Jesus in the heavenly places looking down upon the affairs of men! In fact, let's change this present darkness by calling forth brilliant displays of God's great presence. Ready to do it? Then let's take the intercession plunge together.

How Big Is Your Heart?

John Wesley once said, "The world is my parish." Nothing less than a global vision could have contained the divine call on his life or the spiritual fire in his bones. How available is the Creator of the universe to you? Can your heart receive God's love for His purposes and plans for your generation? How much fire of His presence can you take for yourself—for others? How big is your heart?

When you go before God as a priestly intercessor, whom do you represent? On whose behalf do you stand when you go before the King of creation? The apostle Peter said that we, the Body of Christ, are "a chosen race, a royal priesthood, a holy nation, a people for God's own possession" (1 Pet. 2:9a). We are priests of God—every one of us—and one thing that a priest does is represent others before God.

When the priests of the Old Testament performed their priestly functions and duties, they represented not themselves alone, but all their people. The high priest's garments included an ephod and a breastpiece, both of which had mounted on them precious stones representing the 12 tribes of Israel (Ex. 28:9-29). Whenever the high priest entered the presence of the Lord, he carried over his heart and on his shoulders reminders that he was coming before God for the entire nation.

As believers, we are called as priests to stand in the place of confession of sin and then turn around having been before the King, as prophets to make proclamation in His behalf. When you go before His presence, what living stones are you carrying on your heart?

My father's side of the house, the Golls, come from a long German ancestral background. My mother's kin are the Burnses, who were a part of the Campbell clan from Scotland. Mix in a little bit of English, Native American, a touch of God's heart for Israel—and you come up with my hybrid mix. I was born in the "Show Me" state of Missouri and now am a resident of the "Volunteer" state of Tennessee. As I approach the presence of our Majesty, the Lord Jesus Christ, my heart pulsates in the rythmn of prayer that the destiny of God would come pouring forth upon each of these and other peoples.

FIVE DISTINCT PICTURES

Life begins in intimacy. Prayer is the bedchamber of the Holy Spirit. But intercession is more than just another word for prayer. Intercession is "the act of pleading by one who in God's sight has a right to do so in order to obtain mercy for one in need."[1] Perhaps a little word study will help us better understand this concept.

The basic Hebrew word for intercession is *paga*, which is found 44 times in the Old Testament. Although it is translated as "intercession" only a handful of times, *paga*, when we consider all its variations and shades of meaning, gives us a wonderful understanding of what it means to intercede.

1. *Paga* means "to meet," as in meeting with God for the purpose of reconciliation. "Thou meetest him that rejoiceth and worketh righteousness" (Is. 64:5a KJV). Intercession creates a meeting between two parties.

2. *Paga* means "to light upon." "And he [Jacob] lighted upon a certain place, and tarried there all night" (Gen. 28:11a KJV). That night that place became one of divine visitation for Jacob. By God's working of grace, our divine Helper, the Holy Spirit, stands by, ready to aid us in our intercession (see Rom. 8:26), moving us from the natural to the supernatural and from finite ability to infinite ability, taking hold of situations with us to accomplish the will of God.

3. *Paga* means "to fall upon, attack, strike down, cut down." "And David called one of the young men, and said, Go near, and fall upon him. And he smote him that he died" (2 Sam. 1:15 KJV). Intercession is the readiness of a soldier to fall upon or attack the enemy at the command of his lord, striking and cutting him down!

4. *Paga* means "to strike the mark." "He covers His hands with the lightning, and commands it to strike the mark" (Job 36:32). Intercession, therefore, releases the glory of God to flash forth to a desired situation and "strike the mark" with His brilliant presence.

5. *Paga* means "to lay upon." Intercession reached its fullest and most profound expression when our sins were "laid upon" Jesus: "the Lord hath laid on Him the iniquity of us all" (Is. 53:6b KJV); "and He bare the sin of many, and made intercession for the transgressors" (Is. 53:12d KJV). Jesus fully identified with us when the totality of all our sins for

generations past, present, and future were placed upon Him. Then, as the scapegoat, He carried them far away (Lev. 16:8-10, 20-22).

In "burden-bearing intercession" we enter into a form of this activity as we "share on behalf of His body...in filling up what is lacking in Christ's afflictions" (Col. 1:24b). We pick up the burdens of others, we deposit them before the throne of mercy to obtain help for a time of need. We do not keep these burdens, though; we release them to our gracious, loving Father.

WHEN THE LORD CHANGED HIS MIND

One of the most amazing truths in the Bible is that our prayers can change God's mind. Yes, you heard me correctly! As intercessors, we have the privilege of shaping history before the throne of God. I want to illustrate this by looking at a prayer uttered by one of the greatest intercessors of them all—Moses. In his prayer recorded in Exodus 32:9-14, Moses' holy arguments with God prevailed, permitting God to act in mercy instead of judgment.

At the time of this conversation, Moses was still on the mountain where he had received the Ten Commandments. The Israelites down in the valley had just committed their great sin with the golden calf. God informed Moses of His intention to destroy the sinful people and to start over with Moses to build a nation. Let's examine Moses' prayer to see how he changed God's mind.

1. *Moses argued from the history of God's redeeming acts.* He told God that it would be out of character with His great acts of mercy (see Ex. 32:11) if, after leading the Israelites in triumph and glory out of Egypt, He destroyed them now. Moses interceded for God's redeeming acts, that they would align with His character.

2. *Moses argued for the glory of God's name.* In effect, Moses said to God, "Don't give the Egyptians a reason to slander You because You failed to provide for Your people." Moses was concerned about vindicating the holiness of God's great name in the earth (see Ex. 32:12).

3. *Moses argued from God's faithfulness to His servants.* He reminded God of the lives of Abraham, Isaac, and Israel (Jacob) and of the promises that He had previously given to them (see Ex. 32:13). Moses boldly quoted back to God the promise God had made and held God accountable to His own Word!

As a result of Moses' bold intercession, God changed His mind! That is truly awesome! God listened to the voice of a man and changed His mind! Why would God allow His mind to be changed by the voice of men? Because He has invited us to partner with Him to shape history.

As priests unto God through Jesus Christ we have the right and the privilege to "stand in the gap" between God's righteous judgments that are due and mankind's need for mercy. We stand before God on the people's behalf, pleading on the basis of God's reputation in the earth, His faithfulness to His covenant Word that He has previously stated, and for the sake of His glory being revealed and established. This is the power and the passion of intercession at work.

PARDONED ACCORDING TO YOUR WORD

Let's look at another intercessory prayer of Moses. Numbers 14:1-10 describes how the Israelites have rebelled against God by heeding the bad report of ten of the spies sent to check out the land of Canaan, and by despising the good report given by the other two spies, Joshua and Caleb. God declares that He will destroy the people and begin again with Moses. Once again Moses steps in to intercede for the people. Moses appeals to God on the basis of His great reputation in the earth, reminds God of His covenant promises, and speaks back to God His own words regarding His lovingkindness and forgiveness. Finally Moses reaches the focal point of his prayer.

" 'Pardon, I pray, the iniquity of this people according to the greatness of Your lovingkindness, just as You also have forgiven this people, from Egypt even until now.' So the Lord said, 'I have pardoned them according to your word; but indeed, as I live, all the earth will be filled with the glory of the Lord' " (Num. 14:19-21).

Moses asks God to pardon the people based on His reputation, His promises, and His merciful, loving, and forgiving nature. Look at the Lord's incredible statement, "I have pardoned
them according to your word." God pardoned the people according to the word of Moses! It was the intercessory prayer of
Moses that moved God's heart and changed God's mind. (Talk
about shaping history!)

The next statement is phenomenal also: "As I live, all the
earth will be filled with the glory of the Lord." Many times we
quote this verse without considering its context. This great
prophetic promise of God that all the earth will be filled with His
glory comes on the heels of mercy-filled intercession, of Moses'
getting in God's face and reminding God of His holy reputation
in the earth, His faithfulness, His covenant nature, His mercy and
lovingkindness, and His promises. A bold intercessor stood in
the gap before God for his people, and God listened to the voice
of a man.

God has established a basis for all of us as believers and intercessors to come boldly and "get in His face." Have you ever
wanted to give God a word? Don't be bashful. Remember that
the Lord is looking for people who will "stand in the gap" (Ezek.
22:30) before Him for the land. Let us rise up out of passivity, lay
hold of our heritage as children of God, and with humble tena-
ciousness, "get in God's face."

AS THE WATERS COVER THE SEA

God has clearly portrayed in His Word His desire and intention to bring revival to His people and spiritual awakening to
the earth. His promise is straightforward:

> For the earth shall be filled with the knowledge of the glory of
> the Lord, as the waters cover the sea (Habakkuk 2:14 KJV).

A day is coming when the knowledge of the glory of the
Lord will fill the earth. In that end-time season all people will see
Him and, willingly or not, acknowledge His presence and His
glory. Christ will be magnified and glorified in His Church; and
His name will be exalted above every other name so that every

knee will bow and every tongue confess that He is Lord, to the glory of God the Father (see Phil. 2:9-11). All things will be put in subjection under Christ's feet, who then will subject Himself to the Father, in order that "God may be all in all" (see 1 Cor. 15:27-28).

Are there keys to unlocking the glory of God? Yes, the Scriptures are full of them. Consider the following passage:

> *You shall make an altar of earth for Me, and you shall sacrifice on it your burnt offerings and your peace offerings, your sheep and your oxen; in every place where I cause My name to be remembered, I will come to you and bless you* (Exodus 20:24).

Where will God's name be "remembered"? Everywhere an altar is built. Are you building an altar of worship, praise, prayer, and intercession? In fact, the whole earth is to be offered up as an altar where the fire shall be kept burning and never go out! (see Lev. 6:9-13.)[2]

Pondering on these promises, I asked the Lord one time, "How will You fill the earth with Your glory?" The voice of His Holy Spirit responded, "One clay earthenware pot at a time."

WHEN THE LADDER COMES DOWN

When believers on earth come into agreement in prayer together with the plan and purpose of God, earth and Heaven come into agreement and a "ladder" can come down from Heaven. Genesis chapter 28 tells how Jacob, fleeing from the wrath of his brother Esau, "lighted upon [Heb. *paga*] a certain place, and tarried there all night" (Gen. 28:11a KJV), using a stone for a pillow. (Have you ever felt like you were in a desert and were "between a rock and a hard place"? That is how Jacob felt!) In that very place, however, Jacob received a dream in which he saw a ladder between earth and Heaven with the angels of God ascending and descending on it. Above the ladder stood the Lord. He spoke to Jacob and renewed the promise that He had made to Abraham and Isaac to give to their descendants the very land on which Jacob lay. Then the Lord said, " 'Behold, I am with you and will keep you wherever you go, and will bring you back to this

land; for I will not leave you until I have done what I have promised you.' Then Jacob awoke from his sleep and said, 'Surely the
Lord is in this place, and I did not know it.' He was afraid and
said, 'How awesome is this place! This is none other than the
house of God, and this is the gate of heaven' " (Gen. 28:15-17).
Jacob took the stone he had used as a pillow, set it up as a pillar,
and anointed it with oil as a monument to God. He then named
the place *Bethel* (house of God).

When Jacob had arrived the night before, he had not seen
anything special about the spot. He was scared, tired, and perhaps hungry. He probably lost no time trying to sleep. During the
night, however, God changed Jacob's resting spot from a desert
place to a place of divine visitation. When Jacob awoke in the
morning, he had an entirely different perspective on his surroundings. What he had first seen as a desolate place he now saw
as the "gate of heaven."

What changed Jacob's outlook? His vision of the ladder
from Heaven brought his earthly perspective into agreement
with Heaven's reality, and God's glory came down. Earth came
into agreement with Heaven. When earth comes into agreement
with God's perspective and aligns with His laws and His principles, a ladder can come down and the supernatural presence of
God can come tumbling forth!

Twenty years later Jacob returned to the land of Canaan,
where he had another divine visitation. "Now as Jacob went on
his way, the angels of God met him. Jacob said when he saw
them, 'This is God's camp.' So he named that place Mahanaim"
(Gen. 32:1-2). After living with his uncle Laban for 20 years, mar-
rying Laban's daughters Leah and Rachel, and accumulating
great flocks of sheep, Jacob fled because of Laban's ongoing mis-
treatment of him. The two men had been in conflict for years.

Immediately prior to his second divine encounter, however,
Jacob and Laban had reconciled with one another and then separated in peace (see Gen. 31). Out of the ministry of reconciliation,
cleansing had come. As a result, an open Heaven occurred and the
next thing Jacob knew, he had stumbled into an entire encampment

of angels. Reconciliation between men preceded divine visitation. It always has, and it always will!

GREATER LIGHT; MORE DARKNESS

One of the authentic proofs that God has appeared on the scene is this: The brighter His light shines, the more darkness it exposes in us. I have discovered in my own experience that the closer I get to God, the more darkness I see in me and the farther away from Him I initially feel. New levels of light reveal old levels of darkness. Does that mean that all of a sudden I become worse than I am? No. It simply means that I can see myself more clearly the way I really am—the way God sees me (and loves me anyway!). The sin is already there; the light of God merely brings it into view. Psalm 36:9b KJV says it this way: "In Thy light shall we see light."

While attending a conference in a certain city, I encountered a visionary experience that enlightened me all the more. In this vision, I saw leading up into Heaven a staircase that was covered with white clouds and a mist of the Lord's presence. I was invited to climb this stairway into His increased presence.

Each step I took up the stairs, I encountered greater degrees of His brilliant, white, piercing light. Eventually I came to the top of the stairs and stood on what seemed to be a platform. Nothing but loving yet convicting light shone on this platform. It seemed to go right through me—both from head to foot and from side to side at the same time. It was beautiful; it appeared to me to be a sampling of the "transcendent majesty" of Christ. I wept. I sobbed. I cried out loudly, "You're beautiful! You're beautiful!" I was overcome by the loveliness of the presence of Jesus.

When the electrifying experience was over, two things remained with me: 1) a greater knowledge of His love and presence; and 2) a greater awareness of how darkness keeps us separated from Him! You see, the greater the light is, the more darkness you see!

Yet God's purpose is redemptive! He loves us in spite of our sin and He loves us too much to leave us in our sin. Therefore God reveals sin in our lives because He wants to deal with it. He wants us to confess it so that He can forgive and cleanse us. This was Isaiah's experience. Once he confessed his sin of unclean lips, one of the attending seraphim touched his lips with a coal from the altar and said, "Behold, this has touched your lips; and your iniquity is taken away and your sin is forgiven" (Is. 6:7).

Confession of personal sin is fundamental if we want to realize the purpose and power of God in our lives and see His glory fill our temple. There is, however, a deeper element. Notice that Isaiah's confession had two parts. First, there was a personal dimension: "I am a man of unclean lips"; and second, there was a corporate dimension: "I live among a people of unclean lips" (Is. 6:5). Confessing his own sins was not enough; Isaiah was moved upon to confess the sins of his people.

We each have the responsibility to continually confess our personal sins to God in our devotional prayer times with Him, but He wants to take us further. God wants to release us into a new and higher realm of intercession through identificational confession and proclamation that reaches beyond ourselves and our families to embrace our congregations, our cities, our states, our nation, and our world. I am personally convinced that "confessing the sins of our people"—identificational repentance—is a key factor in removing the obstacles that are delaying a worldwide awakening.

WANT YOUR LIFE TO BE A GATE OF HEAVEN?

I am not satisfied with reading about history. I want to live it! I am not satisfied with reading about "open heavens" in yesterday's great revivals. I want an "open heaven" today—right here, right now!

Do you want your life to make a difference? Then join me and throngs of others who "waste their lives" on Jesus! Remember, time spent with God is not time wasted—it is time gained!

Here is my goal: through the passion and power of intercession, I want to be a battering ram for the Lord that can break through doors that have been shut and burst wide open low ceilings of limitation.

Consider this. I exhort you to get so saturated by the presence of Jesus that you will carry an "open heaven" over your own head. Then wherever you go, you will create an atmospheric change by becoming a "gate of heaven" for others.

A hard task, you say? Not if you know and practice the passion and the power of intercession! Want to shape history? Then follow along with me on the path well worn by pilgrims of former days, and let's shake this generation!

REFLECTION QUESTIONS

1. What does the word *paga* mean and what are some of the word pictures to describe this activity?
2. What were the three prayer arguments that Moses used in his intercession?
3. How can you be a "gate to Heaven" for others?

RECOMMENDED READING

The Lost Art of Intercession by Jim W. Goll (Revival Press, 1997)
Intercessory Prayer by Dutch Sheets (Regal Books, 1996)
Why Revival Tarries by Leonard Ravenhill (Bethany House Publishers, 1982)

ENDNOTES

1. P.J. Mahoney, "Intercession," *The New Catholic Encyclopedia* (New York: McGraw-Hill Book Company, 1967), 566, as quoted in C. Peter Wagner, *Prayer Shield* (Ventura, CA: Regal Books, n.d.), 27.

2. For more discussion on this topic, read the author's first book, *The Lost Art of Intercession* (Shippensburg, PA: Revival Press, 1997).

Chapter 2

THE PAST IS SPELLED IN PENCIL!

W e cannot change the past—but we can erase its sting so that the failures of yesterday do not permeate our response and reaction for today and the future. We are not doomed to repeat yesterday's mistakes. At the end of every pencil there is a handy instrument in red. Just give that wooden instrument a 180 degree turn and wipe out those marks through the red tip at the other end. Yes, yesterday's failures are just a temporary blemish waiting to be removed by the wood cross and the blood of Jesus.

In September 1991 my wife and I were ministering in Queens, New York City. Early one morning in our bedroom I felt the presence of the Holy Spirit come and rest on me. His voice spoke clearly to me these words: "I will release new understandings of identification in intercession whereby the legal basis of the rights of the demonic powers of the air to remain will be removed." This statement opened volumes of understanding to me that morning that I have chewed on ever since.

What does "identification in intercession" mean? What does it have to do with disempowering demonic decrees? I am convinced that it is one of the highest, yet most overlooked, aspects of true intercession. It truly has been a "lost art," but it is being restored to the Church's arsenal of prayer in this hour. Let me take a moment to brush off the dust from this seemingly obscure terminology.

DEFINING OUR TERMS

"Identification in intercession" is a form of confessing generational sins whether they be in a family ancestral tree or those dealing with nations. Another way of describing this prayer activity is "representational repentance." You represent or identify with a people who have done historical wrongs and you repent to the Lord—and at times also to a representative of a conflicting culture or background—and ask forgiveness. Believe me, the Holy Spirit often moves in deep ways upon these intercessorary ambassadors as they are used to carry away the stain of offense to the throne of the Almighty. Identificational repentance is a form of compassionate burden bearing intercession.

Through the Holy Spirit we learn to feel others' pain and unfulfilled dreams and to cry with their sorrows. Our hearts ache out of contrition and desperation by pounding with others' sufferings as if they were our own. As we receive the Father's heart by the Spirit of revelation, in a very real sense those hurts become our own. We identify with God's righteous judgments but burn with His desire for mercy. We feel the crushing weight of their sin and the terrifying alienation from God that it causes. Then, by choosing to identify with them and by laying aside our own position, our hearts are burdened by the Spirit of God. A wrenching cry of confession of sin, disgrace, failure, and humiliation bursts forth from our hearts to the Lord. Such prayer has gone past merely changing linguistic terminology from "*their* burden, desires, heart, and need" to a heart-wrenching "it is *ours*"!

Another way to understand "identification in intercession" is to think of it as a wedding of the spirit of revelation (see Eph. 1:17-18) and the spirit of conviction (see Jn. 16:7-8). The spirit of revelation imparts "wisdom and insight" (see Eph. 1:8) regarding the nature, degree, and depth of national and even generational sin, while the spirit of conviction awakens within us a deep identificational burden for those sins before God—with a desperate desire for confession, repentance, and forgiveness. This wedding of revelation and conviction gives birth to a heart cry for the removal of the sin obstacles that hinder the fullness of spiritual awakening in the earth.

When the Lord finds a people interceding before Him out of brokenness, humility, and identification through the confession of sin, the obstacles can be removed. Then that company of intercessors can be trusted with the investment of His authority and, out of that special place, a gift of faith can be given and a divine word spoken. The legal basis for the demonic powers of the air to remain may be stripped away, the heavens may be opened, and the glory and blessings of God can begin to flood the earth.

This form of intercession is a lost art in our modern-day, materialistic, success-oriented society. I am convinced, however, that the Lord wants to restore it. God's heart for the nations is mercy, not judgment. He is looking for intercessors who will "stand in the gap before [Him] for the land" (Ezek. 22:30). Let's pray for His deeper workings in our lives, so that we may stand in partnership with God in our day as vessels through whom He can pour out over all the nations His compassion, mercy, forgiveness, and reconciliation.

FIVE ESSENTIAL REQUIREMENTS

There are five essential requirements for this type of identificational intercession. Let's take a glance at each of these ingredients.

1. *People who are willing to look with their eyes open.*

We must see the past and present sinful condition of our society. Jesus said, "Lift up your eyes, and look on the fields, that they are white for harvest" (Jn. 4:35b). When we truly lift up our eyes to look, they will be filled with the horrifying condition of the people's present situation. The "harvest," when we first look, is not a pretty sight. But when Christ's compassion is imparted into our own hearts and we know what it is to see and to feel with His heart, then the scene begins to change. It will drive us outside the four walls of the church to see things we don't like to see. It will awaken us to our own helplessness and powerlessness, and from that place of broken dependency we will look up to Jesus, who alone can heal and help.

2. *People who are willing to give up their lives.*

Jesus said, "Greater love has no one than this, that one lay down his life for his friends" (Jn. 15:13). Christ identified with our sinful condition to the point of death, and now He ever intercedes for us at the right hand of the Father (see Rom. 8:34). Likewise, we must be willing to lay down our lives in intercession for the sinful condition of others: our families, our people group, our nation, and our world. This can't be done with two minutes here and two minutes there; it requires a real sacrifice of time, effort, and energy.

3. *A broken and contrite heart.*

King David the psalmist wrote, "The sacrifices of God are a broken spirit; a broken and a contrite heart, O God, You will not despise" (Ps. 51:17). The key to forgiveness is confession and repentance from a heart broken over sin. When we enter into identification in intercession, our hearts are broken over the sins of those whom we carry in our hearts. God responds to broken and contrite hearts; then the rubble of sin is cleared away and the pathway is opened for healing and restoration.

4. *Grace to carry the burdens of others.*

The apostle Paul instructed the Galatians to "bear one another's burdens, and thereby fulfill the law of Christ" (Gal. 6:2). "Burden bearing" is a normal part of Christian living, and it is only by the grace of God that we can do it. Hebrews 4:16 says that we can approach God's throne with confidence to receive the mercy and the grace we need. This verse appears in the context of a discussion of the intercessory role of high priests in general and of Jesus, the great High Priest, in particular. Whenever we enter into intercession we can do so confident in the knowledge that the grace of God is present to give us the strength to bear the burdens of those for whom we are interceding. It is all about grace.

5. *Desperate people willing to be the answer to prayers.*

When the prophet Isaiah had his vision of God in the temple, he responded with confession of both his own sins and those of his people. After he received cleansing, Isaiah heard the call of God: " 'Whom shall I send, and who will go for Us?' Then I said, 'Here am I. Send me!' " (Is. 6:8b) Isaiah had prayed for his people and now he was ready to be God's instrument in answering those prayers. As we intercede for others and become more acutely aware of the desperateness of their condition, we may feel the burden to be part of God's answer to the problem. There is a certain quality about burden bearing intercession that causes us to walk out what we're praying. God gets hold of our hearts, and we reach back into His heart for the grace necessary to pray and act in an opposite spirit.

CONFESSION IN INTERCESSION

One of the most important elements in the process of identification in intercession is confession. Sin is a blockage that must be removed, and confession is the first step. Remember, in this type of prayer we are not dealing with our own individual sins; those should be taken care of during our private devotional times. Here we are focusing on the sinful condition of others—a city, a race, or perhaps even an entire nation.

John Dawson, in his powerful book *Healing America's Wounds*, explains the importance of identificational confession and intercession.

> If we have broken our covenants with God and violated our relationships with one another, the path to reconciliation must begin with the act of confession. The greatest wounds in human history, the greatest injustices, have not happened through the acts of some individual perpetrator, rather through the institutions, systems, philosophies, cultures, religions and governments of mankind. Because of this, we, as individuals, are tempted to absolve ourselves of all individual responsibility. Unless somebody identifies themselves with corporate entities, such as the nation of our citizenship, or the subculture of our ancestors, the act of honest confession will never take place. This leaves us in a world of injury and offense in which no corporate sin is ever acknowledged, reconciliation never begins and old hatreds deepen.
>
> The followers of Jesus are to step into this impasse as agents of healing. Within our ranks are representatives of every category of humanity. Trembling in our heavenly Father's presence, we see clearly the sins of humankind and have no inclination to cover them up. Thus, we are called to live out the biblical practice of identificational

repentance, a neglected truth that opens the floodgates of revival and brings healing to the nations.[1]

Author and cofounder of Generals of Intercession, Cindy Jacobs, brings us additional understanding of this neglected area of teaching. She states, "Remitting of sins is not something that has been widely taught nor understood in the past but which we are now coming to understand as a vital part of spiritual warfare. Jesus modeled this principle on the cross when He said, 'Father forgive them, for they do not know what they do' (Luke 23:34)."[2]

International Bible teacher Derek Prince has identified seven areas or points of confession and intercession that we need to raise on behalf of the Western Church. These points clarify where we as the Body of Christ have sinned.

1. We have not given Jesus His due headship and preeminence (see Eph. 1:22-23; Col. 1:18).
2. We have slighted and grieved the Holy Spirit (see Eph. 4:30).
3. We have not loved one another (see Jn. 13:34-35).
4. We have not fulfilled the Great Commission (see Mt. 28:18-20; Mk. 16:15-16).
5. We have not cared for the weak and the helpless (see Rom. 15:1; Jas. 1:27).
6. We have despised and mistreated the Jewish people (see Rom. 11:15-31).
7. We have compromised with, and been defiled by, the spirit of this world (see Jas. 4:4; 1 Jn. 2:15-17).[3]

This is convicting stuff! Today the Western Church labors under the pressing weight of past sins that have multiplied over decades, generations, and in some cases, even centuries of disobedience and neglect. Church, our hands are not clean! But we can wash our hands and purify our hearts through the age-old remedy of the blood of Jesus!

THE LEARNING CURVE

Certainly we need wisdom to know how to walk in this kind of intercession. There's more to identification than simply changing the pronouns from "them" to "us." Something much deeper is involved. Identification is a deliberate act of the will to join ourselves heart and soul with the plight of other people. John Dawson defines identification as "the act of consciously including oneself within an identifiable category of human beings."[4] It is a matter of the heart, not just of the mind and of the words in our mouths.

I believe in process prayer. For example, God gives us a burden concerning a particular issue, such as abortion, and as we begin to pray He leads us into deeper levels of understanding and personal identification. We begin to ask such questions as, "Father, what led to this sin? What led to the horrifying condition of its being multiplied so much across our land?" As we continue to pray and wait on the Lord, the spirit of conviction wedded to the spirit of revelation leads us to deal personally with related issues such as greed, immorality, rape, pride, and lust. Before confession can be turned outward, it must be turned inward as we let the finger of the Holy Spirit touch us wherever there may be a trace of any of those sins in us.

Through confession comes cleansing. After we are cleansed through the blood of Jesus Christ, we become sanctified vessels, humbled through brokenness over our own sin and able through personal experience to identify in compassion with others who are caught in sin. It is only after we are broken ourselves that God can come and invest His authority into us.

IN THE FOOTSTEPS OF OTHERS

One of the most awesome privileges we can have as children of God is the opportunity to come before God with a broken and a contrite heart over the sins of others, and then to walk in that brokenness, allowing God's heart to be expressed through us. While such a walk may be temporarily painful, it is still a glorious privilege. It is also a sobering responsibility. Because this kind of confession and prayer is a "lost art" in much of the Church today, I believe there is much we can learn from the examples of others who confessed the generational sins of their people. Let's take a quick glance at the prayer life of Daniel.

As Daniel sought the Lord, he began to confess the generational sins of his people that had led to the captivity, even though they had happened before he was born. (See Daniel 9:4-19 for Daniel's complete prayer.) Daniel did not respond presumptuously; rather, he sought the Spirit's remedy so that the promise could be fulfilled. Laying aside any sense of self-justification, in humility and brokenness Daniel confessed his people's sin as his own. More than simply changing a few pronouns in his prayer, Daniel entered into deep identification with his people and the horrifying condition of their sin. Through the "spirit of revelation" wedded to the "spirit of conviction," he understood God's promise—as well as the conditions that had to be met in order for the promise to be fulfilled. With his heart beating in brokenness, Daniel pleaded for God's mercy and for the fulfillment of the prophetic promise.

> O Lord, in accordance with all Your righteous acts, let now Your anger and Your wrath turn away from Your city Jerusalem, Your holy mountain; for because of our sins and the iniquities of our fathers, Jerusalem and Your people have become a reproach to all those around us...O Lord, hear! O Lord, forgive! O Lord, listen and take action! For Your own sake, O my God, do not delay, because Your city and Thy people are called by Your name (Daniel 9:16,19).

God heard Daniel's plea and God's promise was fulfilled!

LESSONS FROM REES HOWELLS

Rees Howells, a mighty British intercessor during World War II, discovered three critical components of intercession that were exemplified in Christ's life and ministry.

1. *Identification*. Howells said that this was law number one for every intercessor and that Christ was the supreme example. Jesus was numbered with the transgressors (see Is. 53:12) and became our High Priest, interceding on our behalf (see Heb. 2:17). Born in a manger, God's Son pitched His tent in our camp, making Himself a brother to all men. He suffered with the suffering and walked the rocky roads that we mortals walk. Jesus was the

epitome of lasting love, and His life defined the intercessor as one who identifies with others.

2. *Agony.* "If we are to be an intercessor," Howells said, "we must be fully like the Master." Jesus "offered up both prayers and supplications with loud crying and tears" (Heb. 5:7b). Gethsemane was the deepest depth in Christ's ocean of agony. There His heart was broken as none have known. Christ's example teaches that a critical function of an intercessor is to agonize for souls.

3. *Authority.* Howells stated, "If the intercessor is to know identification and agony, he also knows authority. He moves God, this intercessor. He even causes Him to change His mind." Rees Howells claimed that when he gained a place of intercession for a need, and believed it God's will, he always had a victory.[5]

CHRIST, OUR PRIESTLY MODEL

The fullest and most profound expression of intercession came in the life and ministry of Jesus Christ. He fully identified with us as our sinful condition was placed upon Him, and as the "scapegoat" (see Lev. 16:10), He carried our transgressions away from us "as far as the east is from the west" (Ps. 103:12a). How did Jesus accomplish this?

1. *He humbled Himself through extreme means.*

Jesus "emptied Himself, taking the form of a bond-servant, and being made in the likeness of men. Being found in appearance as a man, He humbled Himself by becoming obedient to the point of death, even death on a cross" (Phil. 2:7-8).

2. *He took on the sins of mankind.*

"He made Him who knew no sin to be sin on our behalf, so that we might become the righteousness of God in Him" (2 Cor. 5:21).

3. *He lifted and carried away our transgressions.*

"Surely our griefs He Himself bore, and our sorrows He carried...He poured out Himself to death, and was numbered with the transgressors; yet He Himself bore the sin of many, and interceded for the transgressors" (Is. 53:4a,12b).

Jesus, our great High Priest, has given us a model to follow. Just as Jesus bore our sins and sorrows, so we are to bear the burdens of others as priests before God. "Now we who are strong ought to bear the weaknesses of those without strength and not just please ourselves" (Rom. 15:1). "Bear one another's burdens, and thereby fulfill the law of Christ" (Gal. 6:2). The Greek word translated "bear" in both of these verses is *bastazo*, which means "to lift up" or "carry" with the idea of carrying off or removing. It is the same word used in reference to Christ in Matthew 8:17: "This was to fulfill what was spoken through Isaiah the prophet: 'He Himself took our infirmities, and carried away [*bastazo*] our diseases.' "

AN INVITATION EXTENDED

An invitation into divine participation is being extended.There is no way we can add anything to what Christ has done, but we can model what He did. We can take upon ourselves the burdens and weaknesses of others for intercessory purposes and carry them to God's throne of grace. There the Holy Spirit can then appropriate the benefits of the cross, and we can acknowledge and receive as completely sufficient the grace of our Lord and the power of His shed blood. Remember, the stain of the past is spelled in pencil and can be removed by applying the red tip of the wooden instrument.

An invitation is being extended right now. It is as though you are Queen Esther and have come into the Kingdom of God for such a time as this. The King has personally lowered His scepter toward you, and the right to approach His throne has been extended. You ask, "What shall I say before this King of the universe?" Perhaps this closing prayer will help you express your desire before His Majesty the King.

Holy Father, grant us Your heart and Your grace for this deepening work of identification in intercession. Open our eyes to see the needs and grant us Your broken heart. Help us to lay down our lives, grace us to agree with the sin and condition of Your people, and help us to carry their burdens. Make us true intercessors, willing to be the answer to their prayers. Help us, Jesus, to model Your life. For the sake of Your Kingdom and Your glory, amen.

REFLECTION QUESTIONS

1. What does the phrase "identification in intercession" mean to you?
2. Have you ever experienced the "burden of the Lord" for a people different from yourself?
3. Ask the Father now to give you His heart of compassion and the spirit of prayer to be a change maker in your generation.

RECOMMENDED READING

Rees Howells, Intercessor by Norman Grubb (Christian Literature Crusade, 1987)

John Hyde by Francis McGaw (Bethany House Publishers, 1970)

Kneeling on the Promises by Jim W. Goll (Chosen Books, 1999)

ENDNOTES

1. John Dawson, *Healing America's Wounds* (Ventura, CA: Regal Books, 1994), 30.

2. Cindy Jacobs, "Identificational Repentance Through Biblical Remitting of Sins," as quoted in Stephen Mansfield, *Releasing Destiny* (Nashville, TN: Daniel 1 School of Leadership, 1993), 51.

3. Derek Prince, taken from the audiotape "Intercession and Confession," preached at Fort Lauderdale, Florida (Charlotte, NC: Derek Prince Ministries, n.d.).

4. Dawson, *Healing America's Wounds*, 31.

5. Dick Eastman, *No Easy Road* (Grand Rapids, MI: Baker Book House, 1971).

Chapter 3

REMOVING THE RUBBLE—
PROCLAIMING THE PROMISE

◆

In 1991 some friends and I were in Prague, the beautiful capital city of what was then Czechoslovakia. I was the main speaker at a conference that was held in what once had been the largest Communist Party hall in the city. There I was, a little country boy from Cowgill, Missouri, population 259, standing before a crowd of around 2,000 Czechs and Slovaks and trying to exhort them about the prophetic and the necessity of identification in intercession.

Czechoslovakia had a checkered history of conquest and oppression—by the Russians, the Germans, and many other groups—that had left a legacy of crimes and atrocities, heartache, anguish, sorrow, bitterness, and hatred. As I looked out over that throng of people, the Lord suddenly woke me up inside and reminded me of my own German heritage. I stepped to the microphone and said to this gathering of Czechs and Slovaks, "You need to understand something. Goll is a German name. I am German by ancestry. I am the first Goll to return to my homeland as well as stand in your midst today. I am asking you to forgive us, the Germans, for what we did to your beautiful country in World War II."

A trickle of tears began. Then the dam broke. All over the room people started to weep in brokenness, and cleansing began to occur. Then it dawned on me that one of the friends with me was Jewish. I asked David Dreiling, my traveling partner, to come up and explain to the crowd who he was. Then I turned to

David and, as a German, confessed to him the sins of the German people against the Jews and asked his forgiveness.

At that point the meeting took on a life of its own, and wonderful things began to happen. A strong spirit of forgiveness and reconciliation filled the room. All over the hall people came up and confessed their ethnic rivalry and hatred toward one another. Slovaks confessed to Czechs, and Czechs confessed to Slovaks.

I was praising God because I had come to this conference with only one mission. The Lord had placed on my heart a burden unlike any I had ever felt before; it was a burden for two peoples in one country. Communism had fallen and Czechoslovakia was on the verge of splitting in two. The people had to choose whether they would stay together as one nation or divide into two. If they divided, they had to choose whether to do it peacefully or hatefully. My burden from God was that these two different groups would be reconciled to each other.

As it turned out, the country did divide into the Czech and Slovak Republics, but the separation occurred in a very peaceful manner.

REMOVE, REPAIR, AND RESTORE

The meeting that day in Prague is a good illustration of both the practice and the power of confessing generational sins. Although I personally was never involved in the sins of the German people against the Czechs, the Slovaks, or the Jews, I was under a godly burden to identify with my German heritage and acknowledge the sins of previous generations of Germans. The Lord used a humble attempt at identification and open confession to clear the path for reconciliation and healing to begin. Under the leadership of the Spirit, sincere confession and a simple, heartfelt plea for forgiveness can literally work wonders in the hearts of people who are estranged from each other by hostility, bitterness, resentment, and historical, national, racial, or religious hatred.

This concept is nothing new; on the contrary, it is older than the Scriptures and was birthed in the heart of God Himself. That's why I call it "following the ancient paths." Confessing generational sin, although a neglected practice among many Christians, is a key part of the process of removing the obstacle of sin, repairing the breaches caused by sin, and restoring the relationships disrupted by sin. Isaiah 57:14b says, "Remove every obstacle out of the way of My people." In the very next chapter we read, "Those from among you will rebuild the ancient ruins; you will raise up the age-old foundations; and you will be called the repairer of the breach, the restorer of the streets in which to dwell" (Is. 58:12).

In 1989 picks, jackhammers, and bulldozers brought down the Berlin Wall, that hated symbol of separation between Eastern and Western Germans. The social and ideological walls between them, however, were not torn down as easily. In the same way, the obstacles of individual and corporate sin cannot be removed by the devices of men. God has ordained only one way—confession—to clear away the sins that stand between us individually and corporately and between Him and the families, cities, and nations of the earth. If we want to witness a worldwide awakening in our day, there are individual, corporate, generational, and even national sins that must be removed. The only way to remove the rubble is to honestly confess them.

CONFESSION BEGINS AT HOME

True confession arises from a heart under conviction. Conviction is "the state of being convinced of error or compelled to admit the truth; a strong persuasion or belief; the state of being convinced." The verb convict means "to find or prove to be guilty; to convince of error or sinfulness."[1] So confession goes far beyond mere verbalizing or admitting wrong; it is a deep acknowledgment of guilt, a profession of responsibility from a convicted heart, which is a heart absolutely convinced of the reality and horror of sin. I believe that this is a revelatory act that comes only through the working of the Holy Spirit.

Before any of us can enter into an effective ministry of intercession or even of confessing generational sin, we must make sure that our own hands are clean. Each of us must first find the place of personal cleansing. First Peter 4:17 says that judgment begins with the household of God. Confession always begins at home, as we each get alone with God and acknowledge our guilt and our sin before Him. We have to unload our own sin burdens before we can take up those of others. This should be a consistent practice, one done daily or as often as necessary. It is only with clean hands and a pure heart that we can properly intercede for others at any level.

Beyond our personal cleansing, we need to realize as members of the Body of Christ that collectively our hands are not clean. In our sinfulness and rebellion we have allowed doctrinal walls, theological barriers, and sectarian suspicion and misunderstanding to divide us as Christians, in clear violation of the word and spirit of Scripture.

Author and pastor Joseph Garlington in his book *Right or Reconciled?* named 12 distinctions that often divide the Church today. These distinctions are racial, cultural, national, gender oriented, economic, class (or social), religious, "singleness" related, divorce related, AIDS oriented, political, and educational.[2] Furthermore, he adds,

> Paul told us under divine authority that there are *no distinctions* between us in God's eyes. The only reason we can stand before Him is because His Son, Jesus Christ, personally paid the price for our freedom and washed us in His blood. Period. Everything beyond that is stuff that belongs in God's "damned trash can," where you will find Paul's impeccable racial bloodline and fancy theological schooling as well as Peter's temper and racial prejudice.[3]

THE LAW OF PURIFICATION

Another critical key to successful intercession and spiritual warfare is understanding and observing the "Law of Purification."

Then Eleazar the priest said to the men of war who had gone to battle, "This is the statute of the law which the Lord has commanded Moses: only the gold and the silver, the bronze, the iron, the tin and the lead, everything that can stand the

*fire, you shall pass through the fire, and it shall be clean, but
it shall be purified with water for impurity. But whatever
cannot stand the fire you shall pass through the water. And
you shall wash your clothes on the seventh day and be clean,
and afterward you may enter the camp"* (Numbers 31:21-24).

This concept is also sometimes called the "Law of Battle."
Every weapon, every garment, every piece of armor or other
equipment for battle must go through the fire and water of purification—both before battle, for preparation, and after battle,
for cleansing. The same is true for us. As Terry Crist writes, "If
you and I are going to be spiritual warriors, we must pay the
price to separate ourselves through purification."[4] We need to be
purified in the fire of the Holy Spirit and then washed with the
water of the Word—the Bible and the truth within its pages.

As with every other area of our lives, Jesus Christ Himself is
our greatest example of purification and of allowing no common
ground with the enemy. On the night before He died, Jesus told
His disciples, "I will not speak much more with you, for the ruler
of the world is coming, and he has nothing in Me" (Jn. 14:30).
What did he mean by the phrase, "he has nothing in Me"? I think
the Amplified Bible makes it a little clearer: "I will not talk with
you much more, for the prince [evil genius, ruler] of the world is
coming. And he has no claim on Me. [He has nothing in common
with Me; there is nothing in Me that belongs to him, and he has
no power over Me.]"

Satan had no power over Jesus because they shared no common ground. There was nothing in Jesus to give the devil a
foothold or any kind of claim over Him. The sinless Son of God
was totally separate from the author of sin and the father of lies.
Again Terry Crist aptly explains it this way:

The reason Jesus could stand in such power and authority and deal so effectively with the wicked oppressor of the nations was because no common ground
existed between Him and His adversary. When the
devil struck at Jesus, there was nothing whatsoever in
Him to receive the "hit." When satan examined Him,

there was nothing for him to find. Jesus and satan had no relationship one to another, no common ground. There was nothing in Jesus that bore witness with the works of darkness! One reason so many ministers and intercessors have been spiritually "hit" by the fiery darts of the enemy is because they have not responded to the law of purification.[5]

What about you? Are you prepared for battle? Are you walking in obedience to the Lord? Are you keeping your heart and mind clean and pure? Have you been through the purifying fire of the Spirit and the cleansing water of the Word of God? Are you ready?

DARE TO BE A DANIEL

Daniel, Nehemiah, Esther, and Ezra were all effective burden bearers for their people. In each instance God heard and answered, restoration came, and the people experienced renewal. Their examples clearly demonstrate the scriptural truth that "the effective prayer of a righteous man can accomplish much" (Jas. 5:16b).

One day Daniel was meditating on the writings of the prophet Jeremiah, specifically Jeremiah 29:10-14, which prophesied that the children of Israel would go into captivity in Babylon for 70 years and then be restored to their land. The word of God enlightened Daniel's understanding and brought his heart under deep conviction. He began seeking the Lord earnestly in order to know what blockades of sin existed that might hinder or prevent the fulfillment of the promise. (See Daniel 9:2-3.)

Daniel did not just simply assume that all was well. He understood that the fulfillment of these promises was contingent upon the obedience of the people. He wanted to make sure nothing stood in the way. So he gave his attention to the Lord God to seek Him by prayer and supplications, with fasting, sackcloth, and ashes. He "prayed to the Lord...and confessed and said, 'Alas, O Lord, the great and awesome God, who keeps His covenant and lovingkindness for those who love Him and keep His commandments, we have sinned, committed iniquity, acted wickedly and rebelled, even turning aside from Your commandments and ordinances" (Dan. 9:4-5).

Our Father has a plan. It is a two-pronged approach. He is going to raise up more Daniels, more Nehemiahs, more Esthers, and more modern day Ezras—people who will stand in the gap for their people, cities, and nations. Therefore, let revelation and contrition kiss each other and, out of their union, let a new generation of priests and prophets arise who confess their sin and proclaim their promise.

Most of us Christians understand the need to confess individually our personal faults, failures, and sins to God and to ask for forgiveness and cleansing by the blood of Jesus Christ. But then we are called to stand in the gap and lift up an intercessory plea for our corporate faults, failures, and sins including the larger boundaries of our family, city, and nation, both of the secular community of which we are a part and the Body of Christ.

The same is true for the prayers of blessing. As believers in Jesus, we are to identify with our many spheres of responsibility and authority and stand before God for the removal of the rubble of sin and the corresponding levels of demonic darkness. But it does not stop there! We then need to proclaim the promise of hope, provision, and good welfare (see Jer. 29:11). It's time for the watchmen to take their place and shout from the housetops the good news!

PURIFIED TO PROCLAIM

It isn't enough just to remove our personal rubbish. We need to move on in the purposes of God and invoke the heavenly blessing. This is done through the power of proclaiming the "word of the Lord." We declare truths from God's Word and His heart over our lives, families, congregations, cities, and nations. We are to proclaim the will of the Lord. We are to declare that which presently does not exist as though it already does! When energized by the Holy Spirit, the power of proclamation can be used to change the spiritual climate from being a bed of negativity into a bed of productivity!

While I was waiting on the Lord one day, the voice of the Holy Spirit came very clearly to me. His voice echoed within my being, saying, "It is time to make a worldwide impact by calling forth the watchmen to the prophetic power of proclamation." The word *proclamation* means to proclaim, announce, declare, ascribe, call out, cry, invite, preach, pronounce, publish, read, and herald. The time is upon us to release the power of the blessing which is able to break the back of the demonic powers of darkness that attempt to squelch faith, purpose, and destiny. The power of the blessing is greater than the power of the curse! Proclaim the goodness of God.

Jeremiah 31:7 gives us insight into this principle: "Sing aloud with gladness for Jacob, and shout among the chief of the nations; proclaim, give praise, and say, 'O Lord, save Your people, the remnant of Israel.'" Here we have an exhortation to rejoice, shout loudly, and declare that the will of the Father is to bring salvation to His people Israel.

Deuteronomy 32:3-4 NIV adds, "I will proclaim the name of the Lord. Oh, praise the greatness of our God! He is the Rock, His works are perfect, and all His ways are just. A faithful God who does no wrong, upright and just is He." Begin by declaring the names of God over your family and city. Pronounce that your city will be a "center of healing" by invoking the name of Jehovah Rapha—I am the Lord who healeth thee. Declare that the *shalom* (peace) of God will rule over your life and family!

Job 22:21–28 contains much understanding for us.

Yield now and be at peace with Him; thereby good will come to you. Please receive instruction from His mouth and establish His words in your heart. If you return to the Almighty, you will be restored; if you remove unrighteousness far from your tent, and place your gold in the dust, and the gold of Ophir among the stones of the brooks, then the Almighty will be your gold and choice silver to you. For then you will delight in the Almighty, and lift up your face to God. You will pray to Him, and He will hear you; and you will pay your vows. You will also decree a thing, and it will be established for you; and light will shine on your ways.

These verses give us the following ten progressive steps:

1. Remove obstacles through confession of sin;
2. Establish the Word of God in your heart;
3. Cultivate a heart of submission;
4. Receive instruction;
5. Repent and return to the Lord;
6. Receive the revelation that God is your all;
7. Remove of all other gods;
8. Make God your delight;
9. Pray;
10. Decree (proclaim) things that will come to pass.[6]

Sounds good to me! My simple point is that we become cleansed and purifed vessels to declare the word of the Lord, which is powerful to create change in the heavenlies, in turn resulting in change on the earth. Having knelt on the promises through worship, confession, and contrition, we then stand on the promises and declare, "Thy Kingdom come on earth!" (see Mt. 6:10) "What I whisper in your ear, proclaim from the roof" (see Mt. 10:27). We must remove the rubble and then proclaim the promise!

SETTING OUR SIGHTS CLEARLY

In many regions, spiritual darkness has shrouded the eyes of the masses for generations, centuries, and even millennia. There are many strongholds of demonic activity and authority that hold sway over entire people groups because curses, idolatry, immorality, greed, perversion, hatred, and many other sins established a legal basis for those demonic powers to remain and operate. These legal rights must be removed if we are ever to see true worldwide evangelization and awakening take place. We need to set the sights on our gospel guns clearly to be effective.

The second section of this book, "Take Aim," focuses in detail on some of these intercessory targets. Consider, for example, the treatment that Jews and Muslims have received at the hands of "Christians"; how the Church has treated women, not only socially and domestically, but also regarding ministry roles in particular;

how the vast majority of believers have been marginalized by the supposed "separation" between clergy and laity; how the Church in America condoned and in many cases participated in the displacement of Native Americans and the enslavement of African-Americans; and how the Church has in many ways compromised and made peace with a world characterized by greed, immorality, and idolatry.

These sins of the Church have left legacies—sometimes centuries old—of hatred, fear, suspicion, anger, bitterness, and estrangement; and these sins have helped establish the legal right for demonic spirits to enter and exercise influence. Again, these legal rights must be removed if we hope to see global awakening. We must be willing, through identificational intercession, to accept responsibility for these generational sins, to confess them before God, and to seek His forgiveness as well as the forgiveness of those persons and groups who were wronged by the sinful attitudes and actions of our ancestors.

Following these steps can remove the legal basis for the demonic powers to remain and can open the way for cleansing, healing, and the outpouring of God's Spirit. We then reach back into the heart of Papa God and proclaim His promises, which are waiting to be fulfilled. Clearly, our hands have not been clean! But they don't have to remain that way. Let's shake off the dust of immobility and get God's perspective!

To help model these principles, at the end of each chapter in Section Two, I am going to lead you in prayers of representational repentance followed by proclamations of God's will, destiny, and purpose. Let's load the proper ammo of kingdom truth into our arsenal and shape history through the passion and the power of effective intercession.

REFLECTION QUESTIONS

1. What are the generational sins in your region that you believe need to be seriously addressed?
2. What areas do you have in common with the enemy that you want cleansed in the blood of Jesus?
3. What are the promises you can proclaim for your congregation? City? Nation?

RECOMMENDED READING

Daniel by Dr. Paul Yonggi Cho (Creation House, 1990)

When a Pope Asks Forgiveness by Luigi Accattoli (Pauline Books & Media, 1998)

Sins of the Fathers by Brian Mills and Roger Mitchell (Sovereign World, 1999)

ENDNOTES

1. *Merriam-Webster's Collegiate Dictionary*, Tenth Edition (Springfield, MA: Merriam-Webster, Inc., 1996), 253.

2. Joseph Garlington, *Right or Reconciled?* (Shippensburg, PA: Destiny Image Publishers, 1998), 126.

3. Garlington, *Right or Reconciled?*, 126.

4. Terry Crist, *Interceding Against the Powers of Darkness* (Tulsa, OK: Terry Crist Ministries, 1990), 19.

5. Crist, *Interceding*, 18.

6. *Compassionate Prophetic Intercession* (Franklin, TN: Ministry to the Nations, 2000), 65.

Section Two

TAKE AIM!
OUR INTERCESSORY TARGETS

Chapter 4

BRIDGING THE SEPARATION
OF "CLERGY" AND "LAITY"

◆

E arly one morning in April 1994, the Lord gave me a prophetic word in which He said, "*I am coming to wage war against the control spirit and every hindrance that holds My Church at arm's length from the presence and power of My Spirit.*"

The "control spirit" originated in the heart of satan, who aspired to bring all of Heaven under his personal rule. Selfish at its very heart, such a spirit strives to dominate people and subject them to another's will and authority. It even dares to try to seize the things of God and bring them under human regulation and control. This sinful pattern has plagued us as a race ever since Adam and Eve tried to grab God's good gifts in Eden and turn them to their own selfish advantage.

Throughout history this propensity of man's fallen nature, fueled by the demonic forces of darkness, has been responsible for wars, oppression, subjugation and enslavement of entire nations under repressive rulers and regimes; "ethnic cleansing"; and the genocide of millions of people. This destructive desire to control, dominate, and manipulate others is an innate part of our sinful nature and is the complete antithesis of life in the Kingdom of God. Our Lord established His Church to be a community that would live in the world but operate under heavenly principles. Unfortunately, the control spirit has been a problem in the Church as well as in the world.

DELIVER US FROM EVIL!

A few years ago an amazing thing happened to me—I had eight dreams in one night, all on the same subject: the control spirit. In the last dream, I was handed a piece of paper, and I could read the scribbling on it. It stated, *"There are two roots to the control spirit: fear and unbelief."* That dream stunned me as I was awakened out of it. Ever since then I have sought the Lord to bring personal cleansing to me and have lifted up a cry on behalf of the Body of Christ, *"Deliver us from fear and unbelief!"*

One of the most tragic of results of this demonic influence, as well as one of the most costly in its consequences, is the centuries-old separation between "clergy" and "laity." This false distinction has marginalized the majority of Christians in almost every generation, leaving vast resources of human energy and devotion virtually untapped due to fear of entrusting the gifts, message, and ministry of the Church to the "unqualified" masses. Making matters worse, not only have those masses been afforded few opportunities to develop and use their gifts in ministry, but most of them also have lived their entire lives ignorant of their place and position in Christ as heirs of God as well as of God's purpose for them as fully functioning members of the Body of Christ.

From the very beginning Christ's will and design for His Church was for every believer to be a priest with a prophetic spirit on his or her life (1 Pet. 2:9). The purpose of the fivefold ministry gifts of Ephesians 4:11-13 was (and still is) to equip all the saints (every believer—every day) for the work of the ministry and to build up the Church into full maturity in Christ. Sadly, for most of its history the Church has not walked fully in these truths. As a result, the Church's witness to the world has been weak and divided, and the fulfillment of Christ's command to evangelize the world has been hindered. For Jesus' sake, may this change!

How did this happen? How did a Church founded on freedom in Christ and liberty in the Spirit end up bound in the shackles of a control spirit that has severely restricted most of its members from active involvement? A brief survey of Church history will shed some needed light.

BIRTHED AND LED BY THE SPIRIT

From the Day of Pentecost through its first few generations, the Church of Jesus Christ had an infectious, spontaneous quality and was characterized by explosive growth throughout every region of the Roman Empire. This was due to the undeniable living presence of Christ in His Body through the Holy Spirit. In his excellent book, *Floods Upon the Dry Ground*, Charles P. Schmitt writes:

> The most outstanding characteristics of the Church have always been the manifest presence and dynamic activity of Jesus Christ in its midst....And in the first century, Christ was manifestly present in His people! On the day of Pentecost He again came to them from His ascended glory in the power of His outpoured Spirit. By that Spirit He was active in them, spontaneously continuing to do His works and continuing to unfold His teachings through them as His Body....The resurrected Christ, by the power of His Holy Spirit, was simply free to be Himself in His Church! In His Body He freely lived and moved and had His being.[1]

Simon Peter wrote of the Church, "You are a chosen race, a royal priesthood, a holy nation, a people for God's own possession..." (1 Pet. 2:9). The word *you* is all-inclusive, referring to every believer, not just a handful of select leader elites. In the Kingdom of God, we are *all* priests.

Perhaps the most distinguishing characteristics of the New Testament Church were the unique love and unity that bound the believers together. In the Church all believers were equal in their inheritance; they were "one in Christ Jesus" (Gal. 3:28c). No matter what their background, believers were bound together by "one Lord, one faith, one baptism" (Eph. 4:5) in the "unity of the Spirit in the bond of peace" (Eph. 4:3b). They operated under the power of the Spirit, exercising spiritual gifts distributed to each of them by the Spirit as He willed (see 1 Cor. 12:1-11) and working together as many members of one Body (see 1 Cor. 12:12-31).

PRIESTS AND MINISTERS

The early Church understood no distinction between "clergy" and "laity." Any individual believer's position or function was determined by the spiritual gifts that were manifested in his or her life. Since every believer was a priest, every believer had direct access to the throne of God, could interpret the Word of God as the Spirit gave him understanding, and was directly responsible to God for his life and behavior. A priest ministers to God and to others in God's name. The priesthood of the believer means that every believer is a minister. Bluntly put, everyone who is in Christ is called to the ministry!

I believe that the Church was supposed to enable every member to function as a priest and minister. This is one of the primary purposes of the fivefold ministry gifts—to equip each believer to accomplish his or her calling—to do the works of Jesus Christ. But with the passing of the first generation of Christians, a gradual change occurred in the attitude, organization, and governmental structure of the Church.

There were two main reasons for this change: the decline of the manifest presence of the Spirit in the lives of believers and the rise of dangerous heretical teachings that threatened the Church. Of the first, Lutheran historian Lars P. Qualben writes, "The enthusiastic prophetic element in early Christian life was gradually being replaced by a growing formalism in teaching and in worship....The specially 'gifted' became fewer....Instead of the immediate gifts of the Spirit, Christians rather relied on organizations and outward religious authority."[2]

The effort to combat heresy and false teachings was the second reason for the gradual shift away from the priesthood of every believer toward the separation of the clergy and the laity. Heresy was an early and continuing problem in the Church, and its presence caused Church leaders to recognize the importance of clarifying and establishing correct doctrinal teaching so that the congregations could distinguish between the true gospel and the false. This was and of course is an important issue. But when "fear of error" is the overriding motivation behind our reasoning, we will err. Gradually the churches developed the attitude that such teaching could be better accomplished if only one person was the recognized authority in each church. From this it was only a small step to adorning these individuals with official status as clergy (chosen ones) distinct from the laity (the masses).

Subtle yet Significant Changes

The congregations of the New Testament were led by a council or college of elders who were appointed by an apostle, apostolic team, or someone acting on an apostle's behalf (see Acts 14:23; Tit. 1:5). The New Testament pattern was team ministry. So stay with me as we expose and iron out some of the wrinkles in Church history.

Clement of Rome (c. A.D. 30-100) was the earliest of the post-apostolic writers and the first to suggest a distinction between clergy and laity. A disciple of Peter and probably a coworker with Paul (see Phil. 4:3), Clement eventually became the leader of the church in Rome. He was so highly regarded in the early Church that his letter to the Corinthians, which was read aloud in many of the assemblies, was even included in an early collection of the canon of Scripture. Clement still understood a church to be governed by a college of elders, and he recognized only two offices in a church: bishops (synonymous with elders) and deacons. However, he identified these church leaders as "priests," thereby becoming "one of the first to distinguish between 'clergy' and 'laity,' a clear departure from the apostolic understanding of the priesthood of the whole Church."[3]

Polycarp, another post-apostolic leader and personal disciple of the apostle John, became the leader of the church at Smyrna and died a martyr's death around the middle of the second century. In a letter he wrote to the Philippian church he refers to presbyters and deacons as the only officers in the church. Like Clement, he also refers to the presbyters as "priests," thus making a subtle distinction between clergy and laity.[4]

Ignatius (A.D. 30—107), the *"bishop"* of Antioch, while on his way to a martyr's death in Rome, wrote seven letters to various churches in which he took the distinctive step of appealing to *one specific person* in each church whom he regarded as the *bishop* of that church, and exhorted the members of the congregations to be subject to their bishop and to the elders under him. Ignatius encouraged them to look upon their bishop as they would on *Christ Himself*,[5] and that the bishop presided in the *place of God*.[6]

These three examples illustrate the subtle shift in practice that was beginning to take place even before the end of the first century. This evolution of control continued over the next couple of centuries until authority in the churches became vested in one person, the "bishop," without whom no official or valid act of the congregation could be performed. This became the "normal" pattern for church structure and authority, which in many sectors of the Body of Christ has remained pretty much the same until our own day.

I hope it is clear by now that the separation between the clergy and laity was not the practice of the New Testament Church but a later development in a Church that was experiencing spiritual decline. Subsequent Church history is filled with evidence of the devastating effects that such a control spirit has had not only on the Church itself, but also on the peoples and nations that the Church has sought to reach with the gospel.

Left unchecked, a control spirit can cripple and even destroy a church. So how do we deal with it? How can we keep it from taking over? It is primarily a heart issue. The key is learning how to release rather than hold on; how to give back to God what He has given to us. It's an issue of faith and trust and of having a revelation of grace and mercy. These little keys will unlock the prison door that has held and continues to hold hundreds of thousands of God's people at arm's distance from the presence and power of His Spirit. Let's consider an example from the New Testament.

MY FATHER'S BUSINESS

Probably no other people who ever walked the face of the earth went through a greater test of the control spirit than Mary and Joseph, the earthly parents of Jesus. Entrusted with the care and raising of the Son of God during His childhood, they then had to release Him to fulfill the purpose of His heavenly Father. They fed Him, clothed Him, taught Him the Scriptures, and took Him to the synagogue; Joseph even trained Him as a carpenter.

Then, when the time was right, they who had raised Jesus as a son had to acknowledge Him as the Savior. Imagine that test! I think most of us would have flunked that one.

The first real test came when Jesus was 12 years old. It was the Feast of the Passover, and Jesus and His parents had made their usual pilgrimage to Jerusalem. After the festival was over, Mary and Joseph began the return trip to Nazareth, not knowing that Jesus had stayed behind in Jerusalem. Discovering after a day's journey that Jesus was not with them, Mary and Joseph hurried back to Jerusalem (see Lk. 2:41-45). After three days of searching, they found Jesus in the temple, "sitting in the midst of the teachers, both listening to them, and asking them questions" (Lk. 2:46b). Although they were undoubtedly relieved, I can imagine that Mary's voice held more than a little exasperation as she said to Jesus, "Son, why have You treated us this way? Behold, Your father and I have been anxiously looking for You" (Lk. 2:48b).

Jesus' reply was an indicator that things were beginning to change in His relationship with them. "And He said unto them, How is it that ye sought Me? wist [know] ye not that I must be about My Father's business?" (Lk. 2:49 KJV) Don't you imagine that as a father Joseph was cut to his heart by those words? Certainly Joseph loved God and knew that Jesus was God's Son with a divine mission to fulfill, but still he must have felt a painful tug in the very depths of his being. I'm sure that Mary must have hurt deeply inside as well. After all, for 12 years Jesus had been "her" son, and now she was painfully reminded of what she had always known: He was God's Son and had a higher call and a prior allegiance. Even though Jesus returned to Nazareth with them and remained in subjection to them until He was fully of age, the first test had come. Mary and Joseph had to begin letting go of the controls and release Jesus to fulfill the purpose of His Father.

Mary's ultimate test came at the cross when she faced the challenge in her heart of giving back to God that which the one-time greatest event of all history had given to her. As a mother, she may have wanted to hold onto her baby—God's baby—but she had to let Him go and release Him to the Father. Three days later an even greater event for history took place when Jesus rose from the dead, killing death itself and winning forever forgiveness and eternal life for all who would repent and believe— including Mary herself.

RELEASE THE CHURCH AND LET HER GO!

As Christians at the beginning of the third millennium since Christ, we struggle with a legacy almost as old that says that the gifts, ministries, and service of the Church are reserved only for the "clergy"—the chosen, the elite, the trained, the "ordained"— whatever you want to call them. For years we have put too much emphasis on the concept of "going into full-time Christian service" (as opposed to "serving Christ" part-time?!), as if the only people who are really serving the Lord are those who devote all their time to the "professional" ministry. This is a completely false concept that is entirely foreign to the New Testament. Frankly, I want to see this mind-set, which freezes people into passivity and inactivity, be destroyed.

The fact is, all Christians are called to "full-time" Christian service, but this does not necessarily mean a full-time vocation in professional ministry. It means that Christ has called us to serve Him all the time in every walk of life, every day, everywhere we go, and in everything we do.

There are no second-class citizens in the Kingdom of God! Biblically, there is no hierarchy in the Church that you have to pass through to commune with Papa God. We each have a destiny to fulfill!

One of the major hindrances to revival is that we have regulated, restricted, controlled, and limited who can do what in the Church rather than releasing people to function in the gifts, ministries, and service that Christ has called them to. Out of fear, unbelief, and the desire to keep things "under control," we have forgotten the spirit (if not the words) of Jesus' commands: "Go [literally, 'having gone'] into all the world and preach the gospel to all creation....These signs will accompany those who have believed" (Mk. 16:15,17a); and "Go [literally, 'going therefore,' or 'as you go'] therefore and make disciples of all the nations" (Mt. 28:19a).

The "fivefold ministry" gifts of apostle, prophet, evangelist, pastor, and teacher were given "for the equipping of the saints for the work of service, to the building up of the body of Christ" (Eph. 4:12). There are two dimensions here: an internal dimension of serving and building up each other as members of Christ's Body, and an external dimension of serving others in Christ's name and building His Body by bringing lost people into His Kingdom. Success in either dimension requires all believers to be equipped and functioning in ministry, not just the elite "chosen few."

I have a novel idea—let's empower *all* believers and cheer them on to do the stuff. Let's just roll the dice and go for it for Jesus' sake!

NEW PARADIGMS FOR A NEW MILLENNIUM

Now let's touch another "sacred cow" for a moment. There is a long-standing mentality in much of the Church that says that unless you are "ordained clergy" you do not or cannot function in the fivefold ministry gifts, or that you have to be someone "special" to operate in the Spirit. Frankly, that's religious hogwash! I am convinced that the Lord wants to shatter that mentality and turn our understanding upside down on this! Nowhere does the Word of God say that you cannot move in the gifts of healing and work at a bank, a grocery store, or be the CEO of a company! Nowhere does the Bible teach that only the "well-educated" and the "ordained" can prophesy or preach the gospel!

The world will never be won for Christ as long as the anointing stays within the four walls of the church building. God wants to break down those walls and pour out a great "marketplace anointing." He wants to release a mighty army to carry the presence of Christ into the schools, the factories, and the public arena; He wants an army of anointed carpenters, chefs, and bus drivers; teachers, mechanics, and secretaries; doctors, lawyers, and engineers. New marketplace paradigms of the Kingdom of God are emerging as we begin this new millennium.

It is time for the "clergy-laity" mentality to let go of the controls and release all the saints (ordinary, everyday believers) of the Lord into their God-given places of ministry and service. For many centuries members of the clergy and others in the hierarchy of church government have wrongfully repressed and held back millions of believers from reaching out to claim their rightful place in Kingdom work. As a representational member of the "clergy" I say, "*We have sinned! O God, forgive us!*"

To all of you "marketplace people" disciples of Jesus—those who are trying to be "real" for Christ in the "real" world, "*I ask you to forgive us, the 'clergy,' for this great sin against you! Forgive us for holding you back, for not trusting you with the Spirit's anointing, for fearing that your impact could be greater than ours, and for not allowing you to reach out for the fullness of your life in Christ! We repent for the separation of 'clergy and laity' in Jesus' name.*"

Lord, forgive us! Body of Christ, forgive us!

A TIME OF CHANGE

Five hundred years ago, at a great cost, the Body of Christ underwent a radical reformation in the Church that restored the understanding of the "priesthood of each believer." In this generation, we are experiencing the beginning of a "prophetic revolution" in the Church in which God is coming to invade our ungodly comfort zones with His Spirit's presence and power. He is coming with His manifest glory to transform the Church.

Let's clear away generational debris through intercessory acts of representational repentance. But let's move past that into the next dimension of our intercessory position. Arise in faith and now declare with me for days of "new beginnings" to come forth! We agree with our Father that it is time to "wage war" against the control spirit and every hindrance that holds God's people at arm's length from the presence and power of the Holy Spirit.

In Jesus' name, we declare that the Holy Spirit will be poured out upon all people everywhere! The power, the presence and the gifts of the Spirit shall flow freely through every member of the Body of Christ. Bridges shall be built between authentic fivefold spiritual authority and members of each congregation. The nuclear church and the extended church shall work together in cooperation! We declare that the greatest revival of all times is right upon us for the glory of God the Father. Amen!

◆

REFLECTION QUESTIONS

1.   What does the term *control spirit* mean to you?
2.   What is one of the barriers on the part of church leadership that hinders them from empowering the laity to do "the work of ministry"?
3.   What is one of the barriers on the part of everyday believers that hinders them from taking their position in the world of being salt and light in society?

RECOMMENDED READING

Floods Upon the Dry Ground by Charles Schmitt (Revival Press, 1998)
Loving Monday by John D. Beckett (InterVarsity Press, 1998)
Anointed for Business by Ed Silvosa (Regal Books, 2001)

ENDNOTES

1. Charles P. Schmitt, *Floods Upon the Dry Ground* (Shippensburg, PA: Revival Press, 1998), 5, 8.

2. Lars P. Qualben, *A History of the Christian Church* (New York: Thomas Nelson and Sons, 1933), 86, 96, as quoted in Schmitt, *Floods Upon the Dry Ground*, 16.

3. Schmitt, *Floods Upon the Dry Ground*, 23.

4. Schmitt, *Floods Upon the Dry Ground*, 24.

5. Ignatius, "The Epistle of Ignatius to the Ephesians," *The Ante-Nicene Fathers, Vol. 1*. Christian Classics Ethereal Library. 16 August 1999. www.ccel.org/fathers2/ANF-01/anf01-16.htm #P1106_207779.

6. Ignatius, "The Epistle of Ignatius to the Magnesians," *The Ante-Nicene Fathers, Vol. 1*. Christian Classics Ethereal Library. 16 August 1999. www.ccel.org/fathers2/ANF-01/anf01-htm #P1394_249090.

Chapter 5

CLOSING THE GENDER GAP

◆

What general, in going to war, would order 60 percent of his army to stay home? In effect, this is exactly what happens so often in the life of the Church. Some years ago I read that 60 percent of all church members are women and 80 percent of all intercessors are women. Does it not make sense then that we should recognize and release the largest part of God's army to wage war on His behalf and minister to a lost world in His name?

It is my conviction that, historically, women are the most oppressed people group on the face of the earth. Although we acknowledge that this is certainly true in Muslim, Hindu, and many other non-Christian cultures, the tragic reality is that it is also true in the history of the Church. Much of the domination and subjugation of women in Western culture through the ages has been done in the name of Christ!

Great harm has been done to the Church and to the cause of the Kingdom of God in the earth because Christian women traditionally have been relegated to second-class status in the Body of Christ. According to Dr. Fuchsia Pickett, noted preacher, teacher, and author,

> It is difficult to estimate the damage that has been done to the Body of Christ because of prejudice against gender. What giftings, ministries, consolations, and virtues have been inadvertently robbed from the Church because of strong prejudicial discrimination against the female gender. And what overt harm has been perpetrated on the Church because of women's harsh reactions against the limitations placed upon them that

frustrated their expression of the giftings of God in their lives.[1]

CAN GOD USE A WOMAN?

That is an excellent question! Is it not possible, then, that God could use a woman? After all, if we get honest, we are all a bunch of "cracked pots"!

On the serious side, the New Testament makes it clear that women were at the forefront of the birth and growth of the Church. Consider these Bible statistics:

• A Samaritan woman was one of the first to proclaim the gospel when she told the people of her village about Jesus (see Jn. 4:25-29,39).

• It was women who were the last to leave the cross (Jesus' disciples scattered when He was arrested). They also were the ones who watched to see where Jesus was buried (see Mk. 15:40-41,47).

• It was women who were the first to come to Jesus' tomb on the third day (see Mt. 28:1; Mk. 16:1-2; Lk. 23:55–24:1).

• It was women who were the first to declare that Christ was risen (see Mt. 28:5-10; Mk. 16:9-10; Lk. 24:5-10; Jn. 20:18).

• Women were part of the group in the upper room who "were continually devoting themselves to prayer" (Acts 1:14) in preparation for the outpouring of the Holy Spirit on the Day of Pentecost.

• It was a woman, Lydia, who was the first to respond to the gospel in Europe (see Acts 16:14).

Let's continue on our search by looking at some clear examples both from Scripture and from the history of the Church of women in ministerial and leadership roles.[2]

WOMEN OF FAITH IN THE OLD TESTAMENT

Deborah (Judg. 4:1–5:31). Called both a prophetess and a judge, Deborah lived around 1200 B.C.[3] early in the time between Israel's entrance into the Promised Land under Joshua and the establishment of the monarchy under Saul. "Now Deborah, a prophetess, the wife of Lappidoth, was judging Israel at that time...and the sons of Israel came up to her for judgment" (Judg. 4:4-5). This means that she heard and decided cases brought to her by the people of Israel. "Deborah is described in Judges 5:7 as 'a mother in Israel' because of her role in delivering God's people."[4] This remarkable woman truly was an anointed servant of God who led her people with courage and faith.

Huldah (2 Kings 22:14-20; 2 Chron. 34:22-28). Josiah, a godly king of Judah, was in the midst of carrying out sweeping spiritual reforms throughout the nation (2 Chron. 34:1-7). During the cleaning of the temple in preparation for repairing it, a copy of the Law of Moses was discovered (2 Chron. 34:8-15). When it was read to Josiah, he tore his clothes in sorrow and repentance for how the people had disobeyed God (2 Chron. 34:16-19). He then ordered some of his advisers and servants to "inquire of the Lord for me and for those who are left in Israel and in Judah" (2 Chron. 34:21a).

For this important assignment the servants of the king sought out a prophetess named Huldah. Brief as this reference is, Huldah's example is clear proof that the word of the Lord was given to women as well as to men and that their prophetic word was respected, even in a patriarchal society such as Israel.

Esther (The Book of Esther). The story of Esther dates from the time of Israel's exile and captivity. Esther was a Jewish orphan girl who was raised by her cousin, Mordecai, and who was later chosen to be queen to Ahasuerus, king of Persia. At the time of her coronation Ahasuerus did not know that Esther was Jewish.

Haman, the prime minister, connived a scheme to kill all the Jewish people. Learning of the plot, Mordecai told Esther and urged her to tell the king. "If you remain silent at this time, relief and deliverance will arise for the Jews from another place and you and your father's house will perish. And who knows whether you have not attained royalty for such a time as this?" (Esther 4:14) This verse is the central focus of the Book of Esther. After three days of fasting Esther approached the king unsummoned, risking death by doing so. The tables were turned on

Haman and he was hung on his own gallows, while the Jews were saved.

In a time of great crisis, God raised up a woman as His instrument of deliverance. Through her courageous and self-sacrificing boldness, God's people found refuge.

WOMEN OF FAITH IN THE NEW TESTAMENT

Priscilla (Acts 18:2,18,26; Rom. 16:3; 1 Cor. 16:19; 2 Tim. 4:19). Priscilla and her husband, Aquila, were Jewish Christians who fled to Corinth when Emperor Claudius expelled all the Jews from Rome. There they met and worked with Paul in their common trade of tentmaking. Both Priscilla and Aquila were skilled teachers, at one point even instructing the eloquent and persuasive Apollos; they "explained to him the way of God more accurately" (Acts 18:26b). Paul called them "fellow workers" with him in Christ Jesus (see Rom. 16:3), a term he applies equally to men and women throughout his letters. Priscilla and Aquila were active in proclaiming the gospel and in planting churches, even leading one in their home (1 Cor. 16:19). In four of the six occurrences of their names, Priscilla is listed first, which is a possible indication of her particular prominence.

Lydia (Acts 16:14-15,40). The first recorded European convert to Christ, Lydia was a native of Thyatira who lived in Philippi. Her household became the nucleus of the church that Paul established in the city on his second missionary journey. Since all the churches at this time were house churches, Lydia undoubtedly exercised some leadership in that congregation. That she was a "seller of purple" indicates that she was probably wealthy.

Nympha (Col. 4:15). Paul sends greetings to "Nympha and the church that is in her house." Nympha's house church was probably located in Laodicea, and the phrasing of Paul's words suggests that she was a leader of that church, very possibly with pastoral-type responsibilities.

The four daughters of Philip the evangelist (Acts 21:8-9). Philip's daughters are called "prophetesses" and apparently provided ministry to the church at Caesarea. May daughters of purity and the prophetic emerge again this day! And may secure wives like the nameless wife of Phillip invest themselves into the purposes of God in the next generation. Who do you think nurtured that prophetic gift in those four daughters?

Euodia and Syntyche (Phil. 4:2-3). These two women served the church at Philippi, possibly as deacons or as leaders of house churches that met in their respective homes. Paul commended them as fellow workers with him in the gospel. Their influence in the church was such that their disagreement with each other concerned Paul, to the point that he urged them to "live in harmony in the Lord."

Junia (Rom. 16:7). Some translations spell the name "Junias." Either way, the name is feminine in form. Paul calls Andronicus and Junias his "kinsmen" and "fellow prisoners, who are outstanding among the apostles." Early Christian leaders and writers were unanimous in the belief that Junias was a woman. John Crysostom (347–407) and Jerome (343–420) both refer to her as a female apostle.[5] She may have been the wife of Andronicus. At any rate, the fact that Paul calls her an apostle is certainly significant.

Phoebe (Rom. 16:1-2). Paul commends to the church at Rome this woman whom he calls "a helper of many, and of myself as well." He describes her as a "servant" (NAS, NIV) of the church at Cenchrea. The basic Greek word used here is *diakonos*, which means "servant, minister, or deacon." In Romans 16:1, in reference to Phoebe, the word appears in a masculine form, *diakonon*, "strongly suggesting that it is the technical term of the office of deacon."[6] According to an early source Phoebe was well known throughout the Empire to Greeks, Romans, and barbarians alike, traveling extensively and preaching the gospel in foreign countries.[7] Phoebe obviously was a highly respected leader in the early Church.

WOMEN OF FAITH IN THE MEDIEVAL CHURCH (A.D. 100–1400)

Marcella (325–410). An important teacher in the early Church, Marcella actively engaged in dialogue with heretics and brought many into a better understanding of Christian truth. She was highly regarded by Jerome, the translator of the Vulgate. Once, when a dispute arose in Rome over the meaning of certain

Scriptures, Jerome asked Marcella to settle it.[8] Born into a noble Roman family, Marcella turned her palatial home into a retreat for Bible study, teaching, and Christian activities, using her wealth and energy for benevolent work, prayer, and teaching the Scriptures to other Roman women.[9]

Paula (347–404). Paula was born into an aristocratic Roman family. One of the wealthiest women of her day, she nevertheless gave it all away after her husband died and dedicated herself to a life of full service to God. She became known for her simplicity, poverty, and humility. With a solid grasp of the Bible, she often challenged Jerome with scriptural questions and provided fresh insights into the meanings of Bible passages.[10] Paula and her daughter Eustochium directly assisted Jerome in his translation of the Bible into Latin, revising and correcting his translations and making new Latin translations from the Hebrew and Greek texts. During her life Paula founded three convents and a monastery in Bethlehem, where biblical manuscripts were copied.[11]

Theodora (508–548). A woman of great learning and intellect, Theodora was the wife of the Christian emperor Justinian and was widely known as a moral reformer. Justinian was essentially the human head of the Church of his day and, as empress, Theodora shared his powers. Their reign together "was described as the most brilliant of the Byzantine Empire."[12]

Hildegard of Bingen (1098–1179). Known throughout Europe, this German abbess, mystic, and writer was an accomplished musician and theologian. She also was skilled in medicine, politics, and many other disciplines. Hildegard boldly challenged the sinfulness of the great men of her day, both in the Church and the state. People attributed many miracles to her during her lifetime.[13]

Women of Faith From the Reformation to the Present (1500–1900)

Anne Hutchinson (1591–1643). Raised in a Puritan household in England, Anne learned early in her life to read and think about the Bible for herself. In 1634 she and her husband, William, followed John Cotton, their pastor, to the Massachusetts Bay colony, where they settled in Boston. Before long, Anne began opening her home to weekly gatherings of women to discuss the text and points of Cotton's sermons.[14] These meetings grew rapidly in size, eventually even including some men. Aside from being a skilled teacher, Anne was the first female preacher in New England; she probably was the first anywhere in the American colonies. However, her success and "unwomanly" conduct brought opposition from the established male clergy in the colony. In 1638 she was banished.[15] Throughout all of this, Anne's husband remained supportive of her and her activities.

Margaret Fell (1614–1702). Remembered as the "mother of Quakerism," Margaret Fell opened her English home, Swarthmoor Hall, as a refuge and place of renewal for persecuted Quakers for almost 50 years. At one point she was arrested for holding Quaker meetings in her home and spent four years in prison. After her release, she and her daughters embarked on an itinerant preaching ministry. Some years after the death of her first husband, Judge Thomas Fell, Margaret married George Fox. He became one of the most prominent leaders of early Quakerism, and he fully supported her preaching ministry.[16]

Phoebe Worrall Palmer (1807–1874). Phoebe Palmer began her ministry in 1835 with the initiation of her "Tuesday Meetings for the Promotion of Holiness," which continued until her death 39 years later. These meetings became the center for the growing "Holiness" movement in America, which taught and sought Christian perfection through a "second blessing" of God's grace in sanctification. Annually during the 1850s Phoebe and her physician husband toured the eastern part of the United States and Canada, visiting Methodist camp meetings and conducting their own Holiness revivals.[17] In the fall of 1857 the Palmers went to Hamilton, Ontario, where a planned afternoon prayer meeting turned into a ten-day revival meeting, with four hundred people converted to Christ. Similar successes characterized their meetings in New York City and in England, where they preached and worked for four years. All in all, it is estimated that Phoebe Palmer brought over 25 thousand people to Christ during her lifetime.[18] Her ministry laid much of the groundwork for the Pentecostal outpouring of the early twentieth century.

Catherine Booth (1829–1890). Cofounder of the Salvation Army with her husband, William, Catherine Booth became one of the most famous and influential female preachers of her day, delivering her last sermon to an audience of 50 thousand people.[19] The Booths were firm believers in the equality of women in every sphere of life. Even their marriage was based on this principle. Catherine was a very articulate defender of the right of women to preach: "If she have the necessary gifts, and feels herself called by the Spirit to preach, there is not a single word in the whole book of God to restrain her, but many, very many, to urge and encourage her. God says she SHALL do so, and Paul prescribed the manner in which she shall do it, and Phoebe, Junia, Philip's four daughters, and many other women, actually did preach and speak in the primitive churches."[20] William and Catherine Booth declared the "Women's Right to Preach the Gospel," and I say "yea and amen!"

Maria B. Woodworth-Etter (1844–1924). Like Carrie Judd Montgomery, Maria Woodworth-Etter's ministry began in the nineteenth-century Holiness movement and rose to even greater prominence in the early Pentecostal revival. Licensed to preach in 1884 by the Churches of God, her meetings began to draw national attention almost immediately. Unusual manifestations of God's power attended her meetings, including many healings and great numbers of conversions. In the early days of Pentecostalism she was in constant demand as a speaker. In 1918 she founded the Woodworth-Etter Tabernacle in Indianapolis, which she pastored until her death in 1924.[21]

Carrie Judd Montgomery (1858–1946). After receiving a miraculous physical healing herself, Carrie Montgomery went on to become a prominent healing evangelist. Her ministry grew out of the nineteenth century Holiness movement, but encompassed far more. In 1887 she became cofounder, with A.B. Simpson, of the Christian and Missionary Alliance. Carrie was a significant influence during the Pentecostal revival of the early 1900s, and she was ordained as a minister by the Assemblies of God in 1917. Her active ministry continued until her death in 1946.[22]

Kathryn Kuhlman (1907–1976). Regarded as one of the world's foremost healing evangelists, Kathryn Kuhlman began her ministry in 1923 as an ordained minister of the Evangelical Church Alliance. By the mid-1940s she was thriving as a preacher and radio evangelist in Pennsylvania. The powerful healing aspect of her ministry took off in 1947 and continued until her death in 1976.[23]

On a personal note, I remember seeing the last television broadcast of this unusual woman of God. She stated that God had first offered her gift to a man, but that he had refused. Then she went on to comment, "So God came to me—a woman—someone ugly, despised, and a redhead at that! And I said yes." Availability is always the greatest ability.

So What About the Woman?

This survey is barely the tip of the iceberg in relating the role and place of women in the Church, but even this tiny bit is sufficient to show that from the very beginning God's plan has been for women to have full involvement in every aspect of the life of the Body of Christ.

A simple truth of history is that during times of revival women have entered more fully into the life and ministry of the Church in every area, including preaching; whereas during periods of spiritual decline, the freedom and role of women in ministry have become more restricted. In other words, the degree to which women are released into the full ministry of the Church is a direct reflection of the degree to which the Church is in revival or decline.

Age-old traditions and entrenched mind-sets are not easy to change, but Christ is still Lord of His Church. He is bringing about in our day a new release of Christian women into the fullness of their lives as members of the Body of Christ. The ancient walls are crumbling; the rusty chains are falling off; old restrictions are being removed.

A GIANT PARADIGM SHIFT

Well, let it be known that I didn't always have this view, understanding, or application. Earlier in our marriage, my wife asked my permission to do or say almost everything. She even covered her head just to join me in praying for someone! But then God came with His manifested presence and anointed a little five-foot, three-inch package and made her into a holy volcano for God! I am now married to an ordained woman preacher. So I understand to a degree many different angles here. But as for me and my house, I decided to bless what I saw the Father doing.

This is not just something that has happened in our lives and ministry either. As I have the privilege of traveling the nations, I see some overall trends of things that the Holy Spirit seems to be emphasizing. One of these is "giving honor to women."

While in Brazil in the fall of 1999, I was blessed to minister at the National Leadership Conference of the Church of Christ in Pires Do Rio, Brazil. It was a great blessing to be there and to see what looks like the beginnings of authentic revival for that nation. At the last meeting of the leadership gathering of two thousand people, Senior Pastor Ulyssess called forward all the pastors' wives. Then he proceeded to ask the women to forgive the men, and the leadership of the church in particular, for not receiving them as colaborers in Christ. It was a very moving time; weeping broke out amongst the people, and cleansing and healing began to flow. The time culminated then with all the pastors of this national movement laying hands on all the pastors' wives and publicly ordaining them as co-pastors with their husbands in the work of ministry. It was truly an awesome, holy, and historic moment.

So now with conviction and the experience of having undergone that "paradigm shift," I make the following declarations:

Women of the Church, you have been shackled long enough! As a man in the Church I want to confess to you that we, the men of the Body of Christ, have feared you and have clung tightly to our rights, our positions, and our functions. In our own insecurity and lack of revelation we have been unwilling to fully recognize your gifts, calling, and anointing in the Spirit or to accept you as full equals in the life and ministry of the Church.

Therefore, I ask you, the women, to forgive us for holding you back, for not being cheerleaders for you, for not helping to equip you more fully. Forgive us for not valuing your gifts, your callings, and your anointings. Forgive us for treating you like second-class citizens of the Kingdom.

O Lord, we have sinned and acted wickedly! We have wrongfully bound our sisters, Your daughters, and held them back from full participation in the life of the Church. Release the light of revelation, and may change come in Your Body. O Lord, release Your daughters! I call forth an era of the grestest women preachers the church has ever known. May the destiny of God come forth upon each godly woman, in Jesus' name!

As for me and my house—may humble yet bold, submissive yet powerful, gifted yet ethical women on the front lines emerge once again!

Reflection Questions

1. What are some of the reasons women have been so oppressed and hindered from taking a greater role in Christian ministry?
2. In your opinion, what steps can be taken to close the gender gap?
3. Stop right now and begin to confess before the Father the historical sin of the Church of men fearing women and women reacting against men.

Recommended Reading

Women on the Front Lines by Michal Ann Goll (Destiny Image, 1999)

Women of Destiny by Cindy Jacobs (Regal, 1998)

Women of Awakenings: The Historic Contribution of Women to Revival Movements by Lewis and Betty Drummond (Kregel Publications, 1997)

Endnotes

1. Dr. Fuchsia Pickett, from the Foreword to "Part Two: Gender" in Kelley Varner, *The Three Prejudices* (Shippensburg, PA: Destiny Image Publishers, 1997), 31.

2. For additional inspiration from the lives of Christian women throughout history, let me recommend my wife's, Michal Ann's, book *Women on the Front Lines* (Shippensburg, PA: Destiny Image Publishers, 1999).

3. Pamela J. Scalise, "Deborah," *Holman Bible Dictionary*, 1991. *QuickVerse 4.0 Deluxe Bible Reference Collection.* CD-ROM. Parsons Technology, 1992–1996.

4. Scalise, "Deborah," *Holman Bible Dictionary.*

5. Scalise, "Deborah," *Holman Bible Dictionary.*

6. Richard M. Riss, "Who's Who Among Women of the Word," *Spread the Fire*. Vol. 3, No. 5 (October 1997). 8 Dec. 1999. www.tacf.org/stf/3-5/feature3.html.

7. Stanley Grenz and Denise Kjesbo, *Women in the Church: A Biblical Theology of Women in Ministry* (Downers Grove, Illinois: Inter-Varsity Press, 1995), 88ff, cited in Glenn M. Miller,

"Women's Roles in the Early Church," *The Christian Thinktank*, 20 Aug 1999. www.webcom.com/~ctt/fem08.htm.

8. Riss, "Who's Who Among Women of the Word," *Spread the Fire*.

9. Miller, "Women's Roles in the Early Church," *The Christian Thinktank*.

10. Miller, "Women's Roles in the Early Church," *The Christian Thinktank*.

11. Riss, "Who's Who Among Women of the Word," *Spread the Fire*.

12. Mary L. Hammack, *A Dictionary of Women in Church History* (Chicago, IL: Moody Press, 1984), 145.

13. Riss, "Who's Who Among Women of the Word," *Spread the Fire*.

14. Excerpted from Barbara J. MacHaffie, *Her Story: Women in Christian Tradition* (Philadelphia, PA: Fortress Press, 1986).

15. Riss, "Who's Who Among Women of the Word," *Spread the Fire*.

16. Riss, "Who's Who Among Women of the Word," *Spread the Fire*.

17. Excerpted from MacHaffie, *Her Story: Women in Christian Tradition*.

18. Riss, "Who's Who Among Women of the Word," *Spread the Fire*.

19. Riss, "Who's Who Among Women of the Word" *Spread the Fire*.

20. Excerpted from MacHaffie, *Her Story: Women in Christian Tradition*.

21. Riss, "Who's Who Among Women of the Word," *Spread the Fire*.

22. Riss, "Who's Who Among Women of the Word," *Spread the Fire*.

23. Riss, "Who's Who Among Women of the Word," *Spread the Fire*.

Chapter 6

REPENTING FOR THE
GENOCIDE OF THE JEWS

◆

One of the greatest blemishes on the garments of the
Bride of Christ is our history of jealousy, hatred, persecution, and murder toward the Jewish people. The wounds cut
deep; the blood-red stain runs dark and wide. Historically, the attitudes and actions of the Church toward the Jews have dishon-
ored the holy name of Christ, distorted the true gospel, and all
but destroyed any effective witness for Christ, leaving instead a
centuries-old legacy of bitterness, suspicion, and hatred on both
sides. Church, wake up! Did we forget that our Messiah is Jewish?

This prideful wedge between Christians and Jews must be
removed for a couple of primary reasons. First, the dishonor that
the Church has brought on the name of Jesus, as well as the mis-
representation of His character and grace, must be rectified. Second, the destiny of the Church is linked with the destiny of Israel.
God is not through with the Jewish people, and the Church has
not replaced Israel in the plan and purpose of God.

Each of the areas I am specifically addressing in this book
carries a weight and a burden on my heart. Perhaps this one beats
the loudest within me at this juncture in my life. I want to see intercession arise with passion and power to shape the history between the Jew and Gentile.

A REVIEW OF DARK DAYS

One of the darkest chapters in the entire history of the Church
was the period of the Crusades during the eleventh through thirteenth centuries. These armed campaigns to "liberate" the Holy

Land from the "infidels" served as the vehicle for great atrocities that were perpetrated against Jews, Muslims, and Orthodox Christians. Such terrible cruelties occurred not only in the Holy Land, but also across Europe and Asia Minor—in every country through which the Crusaders passed on their way to Jerusalem. The savage, barbaric cruelty and brutality of those who acted in the "name" of Christ sowed seeds of fear, resentment, and mistrust toward "Christians" on the part of Jews and Muslims that continue to bear bitter fruit today.

A tragic example of this is the history of the nations that occupy the Balkan Peninsula in southern Europe. The various people groups of this region—the Croats, the Serbs, the Bosnians, and others—have endured political and religious turmoil for centuries. Ethnic hatred and religious prejudice have been constant sources of tension and unrest, and many wars have been fought on that soil.

I have been to these lands. I have prayer-walked their streets and opened my natural and spiritual eyes to take an honest look. Go with me now on a little historic journey.

In the summer of 1914, the assassinations of Archduke Francis Ferdinand, the heir to the throne of Austria-Hungary, and his wife by a Serbian nationalist in the city of Sarajevo was the spark that set off World War I, which claimed ten million lives. As the kingdom of the Serbs, Croats, and Slovenes from 1918 until 1945, the region suffered terribly during World War II. From 1945 to the 1980s it existed as the Communist nation of Yugoslavia. Since the splintering of Yugoslavia, the nations of Slovenia, Croatia, Bosnia-Herzegovina, and Macedonia have declared their independence; while Serbia, Montenegro, and Vojvodina remain part of Yugoslavia. Now add Kosovo to the list. The 1980s and 1990s have witnessed one conflict after another in these regions. As a result, an ominous new phrase—"ethnic cleansing"—has been added to the world's vocabulary.

Along with my dear friend and evangelist Mahesh Chavda, I have stood in the very spot where Archduke Ferdinand was murdered. I have wept in identificational repentance until my being had nothing left within me.

The centuries-old conflict between these peoples is essentially religious in nature. Many of the seeds were planted during the time of the Crusades. I am convinced that the unchristian behavior of the Crusaders contributed to the creation of an atmosphere that has given demonic powers and territorial spirits a legal basis to operate. Because of this, I believe that there will be no final end to the ethnic and religious conflicts in this region until the Church rises up in true heartfelt representational intercession and repents for the atrocities of the Crusades.

THE RECONCILIATION WALK

But new history through prayer is being written! On July 15, 1999, the residents of Jerusalem witnessed the culmination of the "Reconciliation Walk," a four-year event during which groups of ordinary Christians retraced on foot the routes taken by the first Crusaders, talking with Jews, Muslims, and Orthodox Christians along the way and apologizing for the inhumanity of the Crusades. The date was significant: it was nine hundred years to the day since the city of Jerusalem had fallen to the Crusaders. Participants in the Walk met with leaders of the Muslim, Jewish, and Eastern Orthodox communities in Jerusalem and offered the apology.

The Reconciliation Walk represents identification in intercession and confession of generational sin in action. The purpose of the Walk was to "bring Christians face to face with Muslims and Jews with a simple message of regret and confession."[1]

Everything about the Walk was timed to coincide with the nine-hundredth anniversary of the First Crusade. The Walk officially began on November 27, 1995, with a day of prayer at Clermont-Ferrand in France. In the same place and on the same day nine hundred years earlier, Pope Urban II had issued the initial call that launched the First Crusade.[2]

"Then in the spring of 1996, a few small groups of walkers started traveling from Germany and France, up the Rhine and down the Danube, with others going via Italy and the Balkans, thus retracing the footsteps taken by the first Crusaders.... They...concentrate[d] on asking forgiveness from the remaining Jewish citizens and praying in towns and cities like Cologne,

Mainz and Worms, where so many Jews were slaughtered during the First Crusade."[3]

The Reconciliation Walk is an amazing example of true "identification in intercession." Each walker was equipped with a statement, written in the local language for the region he was in, apologizing for the way "Christians" misrepresented Christ during the Crusades. The statement read as follows:

> Nine hundred years ago, our forefathers carried the name of Jesus Christ in battle across the Middle East. Fueled by fear, greed and hatred, they betrayed the name of Christ by conducting themselves in a manner contrary to His wishes and character. The Crusaders lifted the banner of the Cross above your people. By this act they corrupted its true meaning of reconciliation, forgiveness and selfless love.
>
> On the anniversary of the first Crusade we also carry the name of Christ. We wish to retrace the footsteps of the Crusaders in apology for their deeds and in demonstration of the true meaning of the Cross. We deeply regret the atrocities committed in the name of Christ by our predecessors. We renounce greed, hatred and fear, and condemn all violence done in the name of Jesus Christ.
>
> Where they were motivated by hatred and prejudice, we offer love and brotherhood. Jesus the Messiah came to give life. Forgive us for allowing His name to be associated with death. Please accept again the true meaning of the Messiah's words:
>
> "The Spirit of the Lord is upon me, because He has anointed me to bring good news to the poor. He has sent me to proclaim release to the captive, and recovery of sight to the blind, to let the oppressed go free, to proclaim the year of the Lord's favour."[4]

THE ROOTS OF ANTI-SEMITISM IN THE CHURCH

How serious is the problem? Do we as Christians really need to take such a radical step as was demonstrated in the Reconciliation Walk? How did a Church founded on love, joy, peace, grace, and mercy end up with such a legacy of bitterness, fear, and hatred?

In the very beginning, the Church was exclusively Jewish: Jesus was a Jew and so were all His disciples. All the believers present in the upper room on the Day of Pentecost were Jews, and for almost ten years after Pentecost, the gospel was preached to Jews exclusively. Early Christian worship borrowed its worship style and practices from those of the synagogue. In fact, the Bible that we have today—both the Old and the New Testaments—was written by Jews! Our origins are Jewish. There "just ain't no way of gettin' around" that one.

Gradually, however, the gospel began to spread to non-Jews. Philip preached to the Samaritans and won many converts; then he spoke to an Ethiopian government official, who also believed (Acts 8:5-13; 26-39). Peter preached Christ in the home of Cornelius, a Roman centurion, whose entire household believed along with him (Acts 10). Paul, with his companions Barnabas and later Silas, proclaimed Christ far and wide across the Roman Empire, bringing Gentiles to Christ by the thousands.

Thus, even before the end of the first century, there were more Gentiles than Jews in the Church. Because Gentile believers were not required to observe Jewish law and practices, the Church as a whole began to lose its Jewish flavor. This "Gentilization" of the Church, plus a declining number of Jewish believers as well as an increasingly implacable opposition and hostility to the gospel by the Jewish people as a whole, helped plant seeds of anti-Jewish sentiment in the hearts of many believers.

The Christian Church, now Gentile in identity, became less tolerant of anything relating to its Jewish roots. During the second century, Church leaders began to take an uncompromising stance against anything Jewish. As a result, they began to interpret Scripture in a new way, particularly where Israel was concerned:

- The promises of blessing to Israel in the Hebrew Scriptures were now seen as the exclusive property of the Church.
- God had cursed and rejected Israel, and the Church was now the "true" or "new" Israel.

- The Jews killed Jesus; therefore, all Jews everywhere forever were responsible for His death.[5]

BITTER FRUIT FROM A BITTER ROOT

The bitter seeds of anti-Semitism are clear in some of the
writings of the early Church Fathers. By and large, these men
were admirable in their godliness and devotion to Christ, so it is
all the more painful today to read their forceful diatribes against
the Jews.

Origen (185–254), a brilliant and noted biblical scholar and
theologian, wrote,

> On account of their unbelief and other insults which
> they heaped upon Jesus, the Jews will not only suffer
> more than others in the judgment....but have even al-
> ready endured such sufferings....And the calamities
> they have suffered because they were a most wicked
> nation, which although guilty of many other sins, yet
> has been punished so severely for none as for those that
> were committed against our Jesus."[6]

Gregory of Nyssa (331–396) described the Jews as such:

> Slayers of the Lord, murderers of the prophets, adver-
> saries of God, men who show contempt for the Law,
> foes of grace, enemies of their fathers' faith, advocates
> of the Devil, brood of vipers, slanderers, scoffers, men
> whose minds are in darkness, leaven of the Pharisees,
> assembly of demons, sinners, wicked men, stoners, and
> haters of righteousness.[7]

John Chrysostom (347–407), patriarch of Constantinople,
whose name means "golden-mouthed," was known as a bright,
gentle, sensitive person, yet he was an eloquent and powerful
preacher. He has come down through history with a reputation
as one of the greatest of the Church Fathers, yet he too had a hor-
rendous blind spot where the Jews were concerned:

> The synagogue is worse than a brothel...it is the den of
> scoundrels and the repair of wild beasts...the temple of
> demons devoted to idolatrous cults...the refuge of

brigands and debauchees, and the cavern of devils. [It is] a criminal assembly of Jews...a place of meeting for the assassins of Christ...a house worse than a drinking shop...a den of thieves; a house of ill fame, a dwelling of iniquity, the refuge of devils, a gulf and abyss of perdition....I would say the same thing about [the Jews] souls....As for me, I hate the synagogue....I hate the Jews for the same reason.[8]

Whew! With vitriolic words like these coming from the mouths and the pens of the leaders, is it any wonder that the Church as a whole learned to fear, hate, and despise the Jewish people?

OUR BLOODSTAINED HANDS

By the time of the Crusades, anti-Semitism was entrenched in the beliefs and attitudes of the Church. In the middle of the eleventh century, the Byzantine Empire was the greatest Christian power base in the world. During this time, however, its capital at Constantinople (headquarters of the Eastern Orthodox Church) was threatened by the Seljuk Turks, a nomadic race of shepherds from central Asia who had converted to Islam as they migrated westwards. The defeat of the Byzantine army by the Turks in 1071 put the city of Constantinople at great risk. In addition, the Turks were ambushing Christian pilgrims on their way to Jerusalem. The emperor and patriarch in Constantinople appealed to Pope Urban II in Rome for help.

On November 27, 1095, Pope Urban called the Western Church to arms for the liberation of the Holy Land. For all who pledged themselves to the Crusade, the Pope promised forgiveness of their sins and direct passage to Heaven (no Purgatory). The First Crusade did not consist of a disciplined army of trained soldiers, but instead a mobile riot of thousands of peasants... dominated by superstitions, easily manipulated and desperate to do something that would smooth the road to heaven.

The first and second waves of Crusaders murdered, raped and plundered their way up the Rhine and down

the Danube as they headed for Jerusalem. They especially targeted the Jewish communities, whom the Crusaders saw as the infidel in their midst; thousands of
Jews were wiped out in Europe. Many Jewish scholars
refer to these events as the *first holocaust.*[9]

Nearly four years later, in June 1099, the Crusaders reached
Jerusalem. They captured the city on July 15, indiscriminately
slaughtering men, women, and children throughout the day and
night. The following morning, the "Christians" discovered six
thousand Jews who had fled to the synagogue for safety. The
Crusaders set the synagogue on fire and burned them alive.
Meanwhile, the Muslims who had survived fled to the Mosque of
al Aqsa in the southeastern quarter of the city. The Crusaders
broke the doors down and massacred an estimated thirty thousand Muslims.[10]

Periodically throughout the Middle Ages, Jews in the
"Christian" nations of Europe were faced with three choices: conversion (forced baptism), expulsion, or death. Most Jews chose
either to be expelled or to die rather than convert (martyrs are not
found only in the Church!). In addition, Jews of the Middle Ages
were victims of many other cruelties and slanders perpetrated by
the "Christian" West. Consider these examples:

• *Blood Libel*, a myth that began in England in 1144, alleged
that Jews regularly murdered Christian children at Passover
and used their blood in preparing the unleavened bread
(matzoh).

• *The Black Death*, an endemic bubonic plague in the four-
teenth century that wiped out a quarter of the population of
Europe, was falsely blamed on the Jews of Europe and Asia.

• *The Inquisition*, designed in the thirteenth century to sup-
press heresy, became a tool of persecution against the Jews.
The Spanish Inquisition (est. 1478) sought to discover and
punish converted Jews and Muslims who showed signs of
reverting back to their old religions and practices. Jews were
pressed to convert; if they refused, they were brutally killed.

In the face of such hideous brutality, atrocities, and vicious, outrageous lies from those in the "Church," is it any wonder that Jews and Muslims learned to hate and despise Christians?

MARTIN LUTHER AND THE JEWS

One of the true shining lights of Christian history was the Augustinian monk *Martin Luther* (1483–1546), whose courageous stand for the doctrine of justification by faith in Christ alone defied the Roman Catholic Church and gave birth to the Protestant Reformation in Germany and across northern Europe. Early on Luther reached out in kindness to the Jews, hoping that they would be attracted to a Christian faith that had been set free from the bondage and error of the Catholic Church. Luther had little respect for the Church leadership of his day, calling them "fools" and "coarse blockheads." Concerning their treatment of the Jews, Luther wrote in 1523, "...if I had been a Jew and had seen such idiots and blockheads ruling and teaching the Christian religion, I would rather have been a sow than a Christian. For they have dealt with the Jews as if they were dogs and not human beings."[11]

German Jews proved no more willing, however, to convert to Luther's "brand" of Christianity than they had to Catholicism, which created increasing frustration for the fiery ex-monk. In addition, he became outraged over some blasphemous anti-Christian literature written by Jews. These factors, coupled with age and illness, caused a tragic change of heart in Luther's attitude toward the end of his life, and he lashed out at the Jews in some of the most poisonous words that had been penned up to that time.

> What shall we Christians do with this damned, rejected race of Jews?...First, their synagogues should be set on fire....Secondly, their homes should likewise be broken down and destroyed....Thirdly, they should be deprived of their prayer-books and Talmuds....Fourthly, their rabbis must be forbidden under threat of death to teach any more....Fifthly, passport and traveling privileges should be absolutely forbidden to the Jews....

Sixthly, they ought to be stopped from usury [charging interest on loans]....Seventhly, let the young and strong Jews and Jewesses be given the flail, the ax, the hoe, the spade, the distaff, and spindle, and let them earn their bread by the sweat of their noses....We ought to drive the rascally lazy bones out of our system....Therefore away with them....To sum up, dear princes and nobles who have Jews in your domains, if this advice of mine does not suit you, then find a better one so that you and we may all be free of this insufferable devilish burden— the Jews.[12]

Sadly, these sentiments have influenced "Christian" attitudes toward Jews ever since. During the 1930s and '40s Luther's "advice" was taken to heart and acted upon by the Nazi government of Germany, which found a "better" way to be free of the "insufferable devilish burden" of the Jews. By the time it was all over in May 1945, much of Europe lay in ruins; and six million Jewish men, women, and children—fully one third of the Jewish population of Europe—were dead.

Church, we have Jewish blood all over our hands! God, have mercy on us!

THE FUTURE OF ISRAEL AND THE CHURCH

If we want to see the fullness of God's glory and purpose come in the earth, then the blight and stain of anti-Semitism must be removed from the soul of the Church. God still has plans for the nation of Israel and the Jewish people. In recent years over one million Russian-speaking Jews have left the "land of the North" and returned to the land of Israel. Ancient Bible prophecies are beginning to be fulfilled. An indigenous Messianic movement is beginning in Israel and the nations in this generation.

Does God have a plan? Yes, the destinies of Israel and of authentic Christians are inseparably linked! God chose the Jews to be the people through whom the Messiah and Savior of the world would come. Even though the majority of Jews rejected Jesus when He appeared, God's covenant promises still apply. Always remember, when man is faithless, God remains faithful. Aren't you glad for that?

In Second Corinthians 3:15, Paul writes of a "veil" over the hearts of the Jews that blinds them to the truth of the gospel. In Romans he says that "a partial hardening has happened to Israel until the fullness of the Gentiles has come in; and so all Israel will be saved" (Rom. 11:25b-26a). The day is coming when those of the nation of Israel who have rejected Yeshua, their Messiah, will be brought around. The veil will be lifted from their hearts and they will believe. Zechariah 12:10 tells us that the spirit of grace and supplication will be poured out on the house of David and the inhabitants of Jerusalem.

God's redemptive plan for all people—Jews and Gentiles alike—centers around Jesus Christ, His only Son. It always has. Everything in the law and the covenant—the sacrifices, the priestly functions, the tabernacle and temple worship, the feasts—point to Jesus Christ, whose death and resurrection brought them to completion. Simon Peter, filled with the Holy Spirit, said of Jesus: "And there is salvation in no one else; for there is no other name under heaven that has been given among men by which we must be saved" (Acts 4:12).

NATURAL AND SPIRITUAL RESTORATION

The restoration of Israel, both nationally and spiritually, is part of God's end-time plan for the ages as revealed to us in Ezekiel 36:24-26 and various other Scriptures.

National restoration has occurred; in 1998 Israel celebrated its Jubilee—50 years—of existence among the nations of the earth. Spiritual restoration—the turning of the Jews to faith in their Messiah, Yeshua (Jesus)—will also occur. This also has begun. Through the International Festivals of Jewish Worship and Dance, I have seen with my own eyes as many as 50 thousand Jews place their faith in Jesus as their Messiah in the former Soviet Union.

In recent years, acts of representational repentance have arisen from different sectors of the Body of Christ. Such historic gatherings were held in Ottawa, Canada and Broward County,

Florida, where Christians repented to the Jewish survivors of the Saint Louis ship that in 1939 was turned away from this and other nations' soils loaded with nine hundred Jewish people seeking refuge. Indeed, may authentic compassionate intercession arise.

I am convinced that a major reason for the historic veil of spiritual blindness on the hearts of Jews is the anti-Semitic prejudice of the Church. We must repent for the sins and crimes of the "Church" against the Jewish people. Only through humble confession and repentance of these generational sins can we break and remove the legal basis for the demonic forces behind the spiritual blindness of the Jews and the separation between Jews and Christians.

As a follower of Christ and a member of His Body, the Church, I now openly confess to my Jewish friends that we have sinned against you! Please forgive us for our actions, our attitudes, our traditions, our fears, our suspicion, our hatred, and our theological misinterpretations that have caused you such agony and anguish and hindered you from coming forth into your destiny. I ask you in Yeshua's name, please forgive us!

Father God, forgive us for our prejudice and hatred toward the Jews, Your chosen ones who are the "apple" of Your eye (Zech. 2:8). Forgive us for the Crusades and the Inquisition, for the pogroms and the slander. Forgive us for the Holocaust, particularly for our silence and inaction. Cleanse us, Lord, from harboring these prideful attitudes and actions to this day. Cleanse our hearts, O God.

Give us Your heart for the Jewish people. Remove the veil from their hearts that their eyes might be opened to see and embrace Yeshua, their Messiah! Pour out Your Holy Spirit. I declare that the greatest move of God is right around the corner for the Jewish people. Revive Your people for the honor of Your great name in all the earth!

REFLECTION QUESTIONS

1. Recite one of the historical sad statements of a prominent Church leader against the Jewish people.
2. When man is faithless, does God remain faithful? Give a scriptural basis for your answer and explain.
3. What are the biblical promises for the Jewish people that yet remain to be fulfilled?

RECOMMENDED READING

Our Hands Are Stained With Blood by Michael L. Brown (Destiny Image, 1992)
Your People Shall Be My People by Don Finto (Regal Books, 2001)
Exodus Cry by Jim W. Goll (Regal Books, 2001)

ENDNOTES

1. Quoted from the Reconciliation Walk official website. 24 Aug 1999. www.reconciliationwalk.org/walk/htm.

2. Reconciliation Walk. 24 Aug 1999. www.reconciliationwalk.org/walk/htm.

3. Reconciliation Walk. 24 Aug 1999. www.reconciliationwalk.org/walk/htm.

4. Reconciliation Walk. 24 Aug 1999. www.reconciliationwalk.org/walk/htm.

5. Gary M. Grobman, "Classical and Christian Anti-Semitism," 1990. 11 Feb 1999. www.remember.org/History.root.classical.html.

6. Origen, "Against Celsus," as quoted in Sandra S. Williams, "The Origins of Christian Anti-Semitism," 1993. 11 Feb 1999. www.ddi.digital.net/~billw/ANTI/anti-semitism.html. Emphasis added.

7. As quoted in Williams, "The Origins of Christian Anti-Semitism."

8. As quoted in Michael L. Brown, *Our Hands Are Stained With Blood* (Shippensburg, PA: Destiny Image Publishers, 1992), 10.

9. Reconciliation Walk. 24 Aug 1999. www.reconciliationwalk.org/crusades.htm. Emphasis added.

10. Reconciliation Walk. 24 Aug 1999. www.reconciliationwalk.org/crusades.htm.

11. Martin Luther, "That Jesus Christ Was Born a Jew," as quoted in Michael L. Brown, *Our Hands Are Stained With Blood*, 14.

12. Martin Luther, "Concerning the Jews and Their Lies," as quoted in Brown, *Our Hands Are Stained With Blood*, 14-15.

Chapter 7

HEALING THE WOUNDS
OF THE FIRST NATIONS PEOPLE

◆

On the morning of February 6, 1992, an historic meeting—the first of its kind in this nation—took place in Kansas City, Missouri. Leaders from 50 different denominations in the city met with the chiefs of the five Native American tribes who had formerly inhabited the land. For the church leaders the purpose of the meeting was simple: to ask God's forgiveness and the forgiveness of the five tribes for the sins and wrongs committed against them in years past by those in the Kansas City metropolitan area.[1]

Sponsored by a prayer ministry called Ministries of New Life, this landmark event, "A Day of Repentance and Reconciliation," was the culmination of two years of research and planning.[2] My family and I were living in Kansas City at the time, and I had the privilege not only of attending this event but also of being one of many believers participating in the citywide prayer movement that preceded it. More than two hundred people attended the event. During the meeting itself, intercessors all over the city were praying.[3]

Following music from the choir of Haskell Indian Junior College, a representative of a group called Reconciliation Ministries recited a list of sins committed by the white man against the Native Americans of the area:

broken treaties…merciless plundering of tribal land…
13 million buffalo slaughtered to force the Native Americans through starvation to leave Kansas and Missouri…digging up their loved ones and selling articles

buried with them...instigating quarrels among the tribes...plying discouraged tribes with whiskey to extract from them what little money they had...eventually taking from them all land that had been promised to them perpetually and driving them to Oklahoma.[4]

Brief histories of each of the tribes were shared, after which the chiefs in attendance delivered remarks on behalf of their tribes: the Delaware, the Kansa, the Osage, the Shawnee, and the Wyandotte. Following this, prayers of repentance were offered by three pastors representing the evangelical, liturgical, and charismatic branches of the Church. In response to these prayers, Chief Charles O. Tillman of the Osage, representing all the chiefs present, responded,

> I just want to say that this is a new beginning, and we must not look back. I read a scripture that said that when the Lord forgives He forgets about it. Those are powerful words. And in that, we forgive you, and you forgive us. It's two-sided, everything that's happened in the past, we know that.[5]

At the close of the meeting, a local pastor pronounced a blessing on the Native American leaders and their nations, and one of the chiefs reciprocated by blessing the assembly on behalf of the Indian Nations. Everyone then joined in singing the Lord's Prayer while a young woman from the Wyandotte tribe interpreted in Indian sign language.[6] It indeed was a privilege to be present and witness such an historic event.

OVERTURNING THE PAST

This gathering is an excellent example of the kind of identification, confession, and repentance of generational sin that is so critical today for healing the offenses, injustices, and abuses of the past. Although such a gathering cannot by itself undo the past or resolve all the problems, it is a vital first step. Honest confession, sincere repentance, and a heartfelt cry for forgiveness can go a long way in softening anger, relieving resentment, and opening an avenue for reconciliation. Clearing the air through humble confession and repentance helps remove the bases for estrangement and helps establish good ground for working together.

This prayer gathering was significant for other reasons as well. The Kansas City area has two particularly tragic legacies from its past to overcome. One is the treatment Native Americans received at the hands of the "whites," and the other deals with slavery.

During the decade immediately preceding the Civil War, violence broke out along the Missouri-Kansas border between pro-slavery and anti-slavery factions. Missouri was a slave state, and advocates of slavery wanted Kansas to enter the Union as a slave state also. Opponents of slavery fought this vigorously. Eventually Kansas was admitted as a free state in 1861, but the violence, murder, bloodshed, and lawlessness of the border fighting earned the region the grim nickname of "bloody Kansas."

All these things brought curses of division, slander, hatred, and murder onto the land that in turn gave demonic powers the legal basis to operate. True unity and reconciliation are possible only if confession and repentance are made for the atrocities and violence of the past.

Such events as the 1992 prayer gathering serve to begin the process of healing and reconciliation. Similar gatherings have taken place in other cities and regions where repentance and apologies have been made to Native Americans—the First Nations People—for their treatment at the hands of European American immigrants.

CALLED TO BE RECONCILERS

According to Second Corinthians 5:18-19, we Christians are called to be reconcilers. Just as God seeks to reconcile the world to Himself through Christ, so we should urge lost people to be reconciled to God.

But in order to be effective we ourselves must be right with God, and this means that we must also be right with others. The apostle Paul wrote, "If possible, so far as it depends on you, be at peace with all men" (Rom. 12:18). Jesus said, "Therefore if you are presenting your offering at the altar, and there remember that your brother has something against you, leave your offering there before the altar, and go; first be reconciled to your brother, and then come and present your offering" (Mt. 5:23-24).

If we want to see genuine reconciliation in our day, we must be willing to take the first step. We cannot ignore the sins and injustices of the past. That's what passionate intercession and confession of generational sin are all about.

If Native Americans had a "battle cry" to memorialize their experiences with "European" America, it would be, "Remember Sand Creek!" For many Native Americans there is no greater source of offense and bitterness than this action in Colorado on November 29, 1864, by elements of the U.S. Army under the command of a former Methodist minister against a village of Cheyenne and Arapaho Indians, many of whom were women and children.

PRELUDE TO TRAGEDY

After several years of mounting tensions, by the fall of 1864 a practical state of war existed in Colorado between the Indians and the white settlers. The Indians had become increasingly concerned and frustrated that the whites were taking over traditional hunting grounds, plowing up the land, and raising cattle on grasslands needed by the buffalo. Whites, on the other hand, were angry and fearful over the increasing number of raids by small bands of Indians who robbed farms and stole cattle, horses, and food. The murders of a rancher and his family by Indians in June 1864 had brought the anger, fear, and panic to a fever pitch.

Unfortunately, misunderstandings between Indians and soldiers inflamed the situation until major raids by the Indians on wagon trains and ranches left as many as two hundred whites dead. Colonel John M. Chivington, commander of the Military District of Colorado and a former Methodist minister, was ordered by General Samuel Curtis to deliver up the "bad" Indians and see to it that stolen stock was restored and hostages secured. Chivington was to make no peace with the Indians without orders from Curtis.[7]

At about the same time Chivington and Governor Evans met with Black Kettle, White Antelope, and several other chiefs near Denver. Chivington advised the chiefs that peace required that they lay down their arms and submit to military authority. Major Wynkoop, the commanding officer of Fort Lyon, had promised Black Kettle earlier that any Indians who reported to Fort Lyon wanting peace would be protected and safe from attack.

In early November, a band of 650-700 Cheyennes and Arapahos under Chiefs Black Kettle, White Antelope, Left Hand, and War Bonnet camped beside Sand Creek, as directed by Major Anthony, the new commanding officer of Fort Lyon. These Indians wanted peace with the whites and believed that they were under military protection. However, Major Anthony was not as sympathetic toward the Indians as Major Wynkoop was.

At dawn on November 29, 1864, Chivington and his command arrived on the ridge above the Cheyenne-Arapaho village on Sand Creek. Chivington's latest orders from General Curtis were, "Pursue everywhere and chastise the Cheyennes and Arapaho; pay no attention to district lines. No presents must be made and no peace concluded without my consent." Chivington himself, although a staunch opponent of slavery, was no lover of Indians. Chivington reportedly said,

> The Cheyenne nation has been waging bloody war against the whites....Black Kettle is their principal chief. They have been guilty of arson, murder, rape, and fiendish torture, not even sparing women and little children. I believe it is right and honorable to use any means under God's heaven to kill Indians who kill and torture women and children. Damn any man who is in sympathy with them.[8]

Chivington's command consisted of 750 volunteers, mostly rough, undisciplined, independent-minded men from the Colorado mining camps who had enlisted for 100 days. So far they had seen no action. Their enlistments were almost up, so they were itching for a fight.

THE BATTLE OF SAND CREEK

Chivington attacked around 6:00 a.m., just after dawn. The battle raged most of the day, ending around 4:00 p.m. Amid accusations of massacre and mutilation, demands were made for inquiries into the military actions at Sand Creek. One Army investigation was inconclusive. Two Congressional hearings painted Chivington and his men as villains who attacked a peaceful village of Indians who believed they were under military protection, indiscriminately slaughtering men, women, and children and scalping and mutilating their bodies.

Eyewitness testimonies shed some light on what happened that cold November morning.

> I...saw that Black Kettle had a large American flag tied to the end of a long lodge pole, and was standing in front of his lodge, holding the pole, with the flag fluttering in the gray light of winter dawn. I heard him call to the people not to be afraid, that the soldiers would not hurt them; then the troops opened fire from two sides of the camp.[9]

> I think there were thirty-five braves and some old men, about sixty in all...after the firing the warriors put the squaws and children together, and surrounded them to protect them. I saw five squaws under a bank for shelter. When the troops came up to them, they ran out...and begged for mercy, but the soldiers shot them all....There seemed to be indiscriminate slaughter of men, women and children. There were some thirty or forty squaws collected in a hole for protection; they sent out a little girl about six years old with a white flag on a stick. She...was shot and killed. All the squaws in that hole were afterwards killed....Everyone I saw dead was scalped....I saw a number of infants in arms, killed with their mothers."[10]

> In going over the battlefield the next day I did not see a body of man, woman or child but was scalped and in

many instances their bodies were mutilated in the most horrible manners.[11]

Because the Cheyennes carried away their wounded and many of their dead, it was never completely clear exactly how many Indians died at Sand Creek. Colonel Chivington, in his first report to General Curtis, called Sand Creek "one of the bloodiest Indian battles ever fought on these plains." Whatever happened that day, "there can be little doubt that Sand Creek occurred because of white incursions, government mismanagement, broken treaties and the fact that there were not only 'bad' white men but also 'bad' Indians."[12]

Although there are many sides to every story, most accounts of the battle at Sand Creek agree that as many as two hundred Cheyenne and Arapaho, two-thirds of them women and children, were brutally killed and that many of the bodies were savagely mutilated.

REPENTING FOR SAND CREEK

The incident at Sand Creek still stands (along with the massacre of 250 Indians at Wounded Knee, South Dakota, on December 29, 1890), as one of the most infamous and shameful events in the history of white American and Native American relations. Immediately after Sand Creek enraged Indians went on the warpath, and news of the killings and mutilations shocked white Americans all across the country. No *official* apology has ever been offered. It is long overdue.

On April 22, 1996, the United Methodist Church, recognizing its link to the Sand Creek tragedy through the "Fighting Parson," Methodist lay preacher John Chivington, took an important step toward reconciliation. Meeting in Denver, the United Methodist General Conference adopted a resolution apologizing for the Sand Creek massacre and proposing a healing service of reconciliation. Rev. Alvin Deer stated, "The United Methodist Church delegation has recognized this was a tragedy in U.S. history that needed to be addressed. With the General Conference meeting in Denver, it was the most appropriate time to deal with the tragedy."[13]

John Dawson, founder of the International Reconciliation Coalition, participated in a Coalition-sponsored reconciliation gathering at the Sand Creek massacre site in Colorado on January 14, 1993. Everyone in attendance was a believer and a mature intercessor. He described what took place:

> I suggested that we make confession and ask forgiveness in the presence of the Lord and our Native American brothers. There were many tears. Prayers were heartfelt and deeply honest.
>
> One woman stretched herself out in the sand, touching the feet of an Indian pastor; deeply ashamed she wept for the lost generation that was cut off in this place. The sense of loss was upon us all; the beauty of what might have been had these two peoples walked together in integrity; the generations of alcoholism, suicide and despair that could have been avoided if a culture with the gospel in its roots had exemplified rather than defamed Jesus to a spiritually hungry people.[14]

FOUR AREAS OF CONFESSION

A carefully prepared confession itemized the injustices committed. It covered four categories (paraphrased below), and each concluded with a specific request for forgiveness:

- *Government/military.*

Confession of dishonest actions by government agents and business interests that cheated Indians out of their rightful land and property; government failure to enforce more than three hundred treaties; government failure to resolve the Sand Creek massacre. *"For the wrongs committed, for the related betrayals of your trust, and for the atrocity of Sand Creek, we offer our apology and ask for forgiveness."*

- *Social injustices/prejudices.*

Removal of Indian children from their homes, often forever, to make them "white"; subjection of Indians to

blatant prejudice and subservient positions in society; violation of Indian graves and selling of artifacts.
*"We apologize for these wrongs and injustices, and ask for
forgiveness."*

• *Sins of those bearing Christ's name.*

Frequent attitudes of superiority on the part of Christian missionaries; imposition of Western culture along
with the gospel; economic exploitation of Indian children; John Chivington's unfeeling actions toward Indians at Sand Creek. *"For the destructiveness of zeal without
wisdom, and the misguided and insensitive ways in which
the Church has dealt with you, we ask your forgiveness."*

• *Violation of stewardship of the land.*

Indians, who possessed the land by the first right of oc-
cupancy, lost the right to large parts of their land due to
the greed and dishonesty of white businessmen, min-
ers, and land speculators in direct defiance of treaty
rights; wanton destruction of buffalo herds, the main-
stay of food, clothing, and shelter for the plains Indians,
which, through starvation, forced them onto reserva-
tions. *"For the wrongs committed in the illegal taking of
land, for the government's unwillingness to enforce legal
treaty rights, and for the hundreds of Indian lives taken in
defense of these treaty rights, we ask for forgiveness."*[15]

The resolve of this issue is critical for the future of the American Church.

Reconciliation with Native Americans, especially, is
foundational. There is a hindrance to God's blessing
on this nation as long as this wound remains un-
healed. Without the embrace and blessing of the "host"
people, Americans will fall short of apprehending
both their identity and their destiny...If the American
Church is ever to reach its full potential, reconciliation
between European Americans and Native Americans
is non-negotiable.[16]

THE MACEDONIAN CALL

The Massachusetts Bay Colony, established by the Puritans in 1630, adopted a seal that pictured a Native American saying, "Come over and help us," a direct reference to Paul's "Macedonian call" in Acts 16:9-10. Conversion of Native Americans to Christ was a specific goal written into the charters of early New England settlements. Cultural clashes, pervading attitudes of "superiority" on the part of the Europeans, and general resistance to conversion on the part of the Indians caused problems from the outset. There were some bright lights, however.

John Eliot (1604–1690), a Puritan minister educated in England at Cambridge University, arrived in Boston in 1631. Together with family and friends from England, he organized the First Church of Roxbury, Massachusetts, in 1632, which he pastored for 58 years. Two years into this ministry, Eliot began working among the Algonquin Indians. His many years of hard, diligent labor to reach them for Christ earned him the title, "Apostle to the Indians." He even learned their language so he could preach Christ to them without an interpreter. As a result, many Indians came to Christ, and Eliot helped them establish villages where more than one thousand "Praying Indians" lived and learned about the Lord. He issued a series of "Eliot's Indian Tracts" to help the Indians grow in the faith. Eliot's most significant contribution, however, was his eight-year effort to translate the Bible into Algonquin. When it appeared in 1663, it was the first complete Bible of any kind published in the New World.[17]

Although frail and sickly for most of his short life, *David Brainerd* (1718–1747) was a bright light for Christ among the Indians of New York, New Jersey, and eastern Pennsylvania. Converted to Christ while a student at Yale University, Brainerd began his ministry among the Indians in April 1743. In 4½ short years of missionary work before tuberculosis took his life at the age of 29, Brainerd sought to master the language and culture of the Indians and traveled hundreds of miles through forests and over mountains on horseback and on foot to preach and minister to them. He spent literally hours at a time, day after day, in prayer for the Indians—often standing or kneeling in the snow. It is thought that by the end of his brief ministry as many as one-sixth of the Indian population within the scope of his influence had been won to Christ.

An 1833 issue of the *Christian Advocate and Journal* tells the story of four Indians from west of the Rocky Mountains who traveled three thousand miles to St. Louis. Why? They had heard that the white people knew the proper way to worship the Great Spirit and that they had a book that contained directions. Two of the Indians dropped dead from disease and exhaustion as soon as they reached the city, but the other two were well received and treated in high style. At the end of their visit, one of the Indians, named Ta-Wis-Sis-Sim-Nim, said these words:

> My people sent me to get the white man's Book of Heaven. You took me where you allow your women to dance, as we do not ours, and the Book was not there. You showed me images of the Great Spirit and pictures of the Good Land beyond, but the Book was not among them to tell me the way. I am going back the long trail to my people in the dark land. You make my feet heavy with gifts, and my moccasins will grow old in carrying them, and yet the Book is not among them. When I tell my poor, blind people, after one more snow, in the big council, that I did not bring the Book, no word will be spoken by our old men or by our young braves. One by one, they will rise up and go out in silence. My people will die in darkness, and they will go a long path to other hunting grounds. No white man will go with them, and no white man's Book to make the way plain. I have no more words.[18]

Talk about a "Macedonian call"! What a marvelous opportunity! What a tragic failure! The appearance of these words convicted many of God's people, and about one a hundred missionaries answered the call to take the gospel to the Indians. May we learn from the past to humbly seize the day of opportunity.

A Humble Confession

As a white American Christian of European descent, I ask the First Nations People—the Native American brothers and sisters—to forgive us for our colonialization, for our prideful entry, for our cultural arrogance! Forgive us for the exploitation, the lies, the betrayal, the murder, the theft of your land, the destruction of your way of life, and the contempt for your dignity! Forgive us for showing you a Christianity without love, a "form of godliness" but without its power; for talking about the way, but not showing you the way. We have sinned!

> *Father, lift the burden and stain of injustice we bear for our sins against our Native American brethren. Forgive us for our fear, prejudice, and pride. Help us together to heal the wounds and build bridges and move as one people into the destiny we share as Your children!*
>
> *O Lord, raise up again in this generation your John Eliots and David Brainerds! Raise up again among them faithful ambassadors for Christ of their own. I release a true apostolic and prophetic anointing upon the First Nations people.*

REFLECTION QUESTIONS

1. What is one of the great historical wounds in America's history against the First Nations People?
2. What sins committed against the Native North American Indians do you believe you could begin to confess before the Father in behalf of our (your) nation?
3. If you stood right now before one of the First Nations People, what would you have to say as a Christian?

RECOMMENDED READING

Healing America's Wounds by John Dawson (Regal, 1994)
Can You Feel the Mountains Tremble? A Healing the Land Handbook by Dr. Suugiina (Inuit Ministries International, 1999)
One Church, Many Tribes by Richard Twiss (Regal Books, 2000)

ENDNOTES

1. Albert Rountree, "Why Should We Christians Repent for the Sins Committed by Others in Years Past?" *New Life* newsletter (Ministries of New Life, n.d.), 5.

2. Bette Armstrong, "A Day of Repentance and Reconciliation," *New Life* newsletter (Ministries of New Life, n.d.), 1.

3. Armstrong, "A Day of Repentance and Reconciliation," *New Life* newsletter, 1.

4. Armstrong, "A Day of Repentance and Reconciliation," *New Life* newsletter, 2.

5. Armstrong, "A Day of Repentance and Reconciliation," *New Life* newsletter, 4.

6. Armstrong, "A Day of Repentance and Reconciliation," *New Life* newsletter, 4.

7. J. Jay Myers, "The Notorious Fight at Sand Creek," *WildWest*, December, 1998. 2 Feb 1999. www.thehistorynet.com/WildWest/articles/1998/1298_text.htm.

8. Myers, "The Notorious Fight at Sand Creek," *WildWest*.

9. George Bent to George E. Hyde, April 14, 1906 (Coe Collection, Yale University), as quoted in John Dawson, *Healing America's Wounds* (Ventura, CA: Regal Books, 1994), 146.

10. Robert Bent, U.S. Congress 39th 2nd session, Senate Report 156, pages 73, 96, as quoted in Dawson, *Healing America's Wounds*, 146-147.

11. Lieutenant James Conner, U.S. Congress 39th 2nd session, Senate Report 156, page 53, as quoted in Dawson, *Healing America's Wounds*, 147.

12. Myers, "The Notorious Fight at Sand Creek," *WildWest*.

13. "Delegates Apologize for 1864 Sand Creek Massacre led by Methodist Lay Preacher," United Methodist Daily News, April 22, 1996. 1 Sep 1999. www.umc.org/gencon/news/massacre.html.

14. Dawson, *Healing America's Wounds*, 148.

15. Dawson, *Healing America's Wounds*, 151-154.

16. John Dawson, "Happy Trails or Trail of Tears?" *Reconciliation Wednesday, A Weekly Forum on Current Issues*, June 12, 1996. 8 Feb 1999. www.execpc.com/logos/eliot.htm.

17. "The Eliot Indian Bible," *Logos Christian Resource Pages*. 2 Sept 1999. www.execpc.com/logos/eliot.htm.

18. "A Call for Missionaries," taken from *A Voice in the Wilderness*, March, 1998. 2 Sept 1999. www.worldmissions.org/clipper/Missions/ACallForMissionaries.html.

Chapter 8

DELIVERANCE FROM RACISM

◆

C hrist wants His Church to walk in the same unity that
He enjoys with the Father. Perfect harmony exists within the Godhead; there is a complete oneness between Father, Son,
and Holy Spirit. No competition, jealousy, or pushing for position there! And that is how the Godhead wants us to walk with
each other. It is time to look under our rugs and see what we
have attempted to hide for years. Under the rug of the great American experiment, you will find the debris of racism, pride, and
prejudice.

Clearly the unity of all believers is both the burning desire
and the demand of our Lord. Yet today there are many things
that we have allowed to separate us into different camps. From
the very beginning satan has followed a strategy of "divide and
conquer" to cripple the Church. His intention has been to trip us
up and cause us to fight among ourselves instead of focusing on
the commission that Christ gave us to make disciples of all nations. We are divided over theology, doctrine, and denominational
perspectives—as well as over baptismal methodology, communion, and spiritual gifts. Worse still, however, is that we are divided along racial lines.

Excuse me, Sunday is still the most segregated day in
America!

RACISM: A DEADLY DISEASE

Racism is probably the most virulent malignancy infecting
American society today, with black-white antagonism being its
most potent form. From 1619, when the first 20 African slaves

were sold in Jamestown, Virginia, until the end of the Civil War nearly 250 years later, the ugly specter of slavery cast a grim shadow over our land. Although President Abraham Lincoln's Emancipation Proclamation of 1863, the Union victory in 1865, and passage of the thirteenth Amendment to the Constitution in December 1865 secured the physical freedom of the slaves, the "Jim Crow" laws passed and enforced by the white majority effectively kept black Americans bound politically, socially, and economically for another century. The Civil Rights movement of the 1950s and '60s brought an end to the dominance of "Jim Crow," but more than 30 years later many of the dreams and goals of African-Americans for complete equality remain dreadfully unfulfilled.

The sin and injustice of white-black racism in general, and slavery in particular, has had devastating effects on both sides. For many blacks it has created a legacy of bitterness, anger, hopelessness, and despair. This is seen most clearly in the cycles of poverty, crime, and broken homes in the inner cities of our major urban areas. Writing from the African-American perspective, pastor and author Michael Goings states,

> We battle an ethnic inferiority complex developed over several hundred years of dehumanizing slavery, subsequent racism, segregation, and discrimination. As a result, most African-Americans face a formidable battle to find equality in their own minds—a fight many lose before they ever reach the marketplace or job site.[1]

On the other hand, many whites struggle with feelings of guilt, self-inflicted or otherwise. Sometimes it is guilt by association: "I'm guilty because I'm white," which often leads to attitudes of defensiveness, resentment, and self-protection. In their extreme form, these attitudes are reflected in the vehemence of white supremacist groups and in the rise of white-against-black "hate crimes."

The evil seed of racism bears bitter fruit. As Michael Goings writes,

Racism is the mother of bigotry, discrimination, "Jim Crowism" (discrimination against African Americans by "legal" means or sanctions), Nazism, the "white supremacy" movement, anti-Semitism, apartheid, and the Black Muslim movement. All of these belief systems and ideologies spring from an attitude of superiority over others who are different....This same evil and deep-rooted belief is still ingrained in the minds of many whites in America and South Africa, respectively perpetuating discrimination and apartheid in these nations.[2]

Racism is based on ignorance. Ignorance breeds fear, which gives birth to hatred. All of these—ignorance, fear, and hatred—are contrary to the will and the Spirit of God. As pastor and author Kelley Varner writes,

God hates racism in any form—it is sin. Racism is rooted in degeneracy, pride, superior attitudes, ignorance, and fear. Unregenerate Adamic flesh is the soil from which racism springs. Included here are pride of place (social status), pride of face (physical attributes), pride of grace (religious or denominational traditions), and pride of race (based on skin color or ethnicity).[3]

Michael Goings defines racism as "racial attitudes, beliefs, and false concepts of ethnic superiority," and has identified three forms of racism according to their sources:[4]

1. *Hereditary racism.*
Racist attitudes passed down from parent to child, from one generation to the next, often in the guise of religious instruction.

2. *Environmental racism.*
Racist attitudes caused by the overpowering influence of one's environment and association (such as hate groups and racist organizations).

3. *Reactionary/reverse racism.*
Racist attitudes triggered in a suppressed minority by ill treatment and acts of racism inflicted by members of other dominant groups.

The divisiveness and destructiveness of racism in our land should cut to the heart of every sensitive and reasonable American, regardless of race. As believers, we are responsible in large part for these atrocities, since throughout our nation's history many segments of the American Church have aided the existence and perpetuation of racism in our land. But we have been given the ministry of reconciliation. Therefore, to my fellow white brothers and sisters I say, "Our hands are not clean! May we change our ways!"

SLAVERY: AMERICA'S NATIONAL SHAME

From 1619, when the first slaves stood on the block in Jamestown, Virginia, until 1807, when the United States banned the further importation of slaves, well over three million African men, women, and children were brought to these shores against their will and sold into lives of permanent servitude. Stolen from their homes and families, these captives were crammed aboard ships especially fitted out to transport as many slaves as possible. Flat on their backs, shackled hand and foot with no space between them, and unable to move, the slaves were often forced to lie in their own excrement for days at a time during a voyage lasting several weeks. In the heat, stale air, and accumulated filth, hundreds of thousands did not survive the trip. Those who died were simply and unceremoniously dumped over the side like so much driftwood.

Those slaves who lived to stand on the auction block faced a bleak future with little hope. Terrified and unable to speak the language of their captors, they had no rights, no redress under the law, and no one to stand for them. Even family ties meant nothing; countless times families were torn apart as children, and even husbands and wives, were sold to different owners, never to see each other again. All children born to slaves were automatically considered slaves as well. Unless they escaped, were able to buy their freedom, or were freed by their masters, slaves were in bondage for life. Because they were "property," slaves could be willed to successive generations of owners.

Slave life was hard, particularly on the Southern plantations. The majority of slaves were field hands who labored from sunrise to sunset six days a week and sometimes seven. Punishment for infractions was often harsh and terribly brutal. Runaway slaves who were recaptured usually faced at least a severe whipping. Sometimes they were maimed in a manner that would make it difficult for them to run away again. Another punishment was to be "sold down the river"—sold to another owner—which usually meant an even worse situation for the slave.

Although in the beginning slavery existed in both northern and southern states, strong abolitionist sentiment arose, particularly in the North. Even though states north of the Mason-Dixon line gradually abolished slavery, federal laws continued to support the institution until the Civil War. A Fugitive Slave law, passed in 1793, provided for the return of runaway slaves to their owners from any state into which they had fled, even if that state was a free state. The Missouri Compromise of 1820 admitted my home state of Missouri to the Union as a slave state, Maine as a free state, and outlawed slavery in every state or territory (except Missouri) north of 36° 30′ latitude.

As northern states eventually abolished slavery altogether, they also relaxed enforcement of the 1793 Fugitive Slave law. The Underground Railroad also did much to nullify the effects of the law. The Compromise of 1850 admitted California as a slave state and abolished slavery in the District of Columbia. It also strengthened the 1793 Fugitive Slave law by stating that since slaves were officially property and that ownership of property extended across state lines, slave owners were within their rights to cross state lines in order to retrieve their runaway slaves. One consequence of this law was that it became much easier to capture blacks, ex-slaves or not, and ship them south in chains. In this way many "free" blacks were charged with being runaways and taken into bondage. The U.S. Supreme Court upheld this trend in its 1857 Dred Scott decision, ruling that slaves were property, even if they were living in a free state, and that Congress had no authority to forbid slaveholding. The whole slavery issue was decided permanently just a few years later in the fiery cauldron of the Civil War, at the total cost of 562,130 dead and 418,206 wounded.

THE BLINDNESS OF THE WHITE AMERICAN CHURCH

Now hold onto your hat, because I'm about to make some weighty statements. The enslavement of African-Americans for nearly 250 years, and their subsequent disfranchisement socially, politically, and economically, remains one of the greatest "generational sins" of America. Confession and repentance on this issue are doubly important for we who are Caucasian American Christians because, to a great degree, the white Church in America has been very cooperative, first in the legitimization of slavery and second in the perpetuation of racial stereotypes and segregation. We stand guilty!

One of the reasons so many white Americans accepted slavery for so long is that many churches supported it in their teaching. There were notable exceptions, of course. For example, the Quakers were adamantly opposed to slavery on spiritual and moral grounds, as were the Mennonites and many other groups and individuals. In general, the people and churches of the more industrialized northern United States were less inclined to support slavery than those in the South. The agriculturally based economy of the southern states depended heavily on slave labor. Slavery was knit into the very social, economic, and religious framework of Southern culture. Southern churches acknowledged the "necessity" of the "peculiar institution." Southern preachers supported slavery on supposed scriptural grounds. Typical of their "biblical" arguments were these:

- Slavery was an accepted reality in the Bible, in both the Old and New Testaments. Jesus, Paul, Peter, John, and other biblical leaders, teachers, and writers had ample opportunity to denounce slavery if it was so evil, yet they did not. Therefore, it is an acceptable practice.
- Africans were inherently inferior, created by God specifically as a "servant race." Among other things, this was based on the supposed "curse of Ham," one of Noah's sons, through whom the Negro "race" is descended.

- Because they were "inferior," the Negro race needed for their own good the regulation, control, and guidance of the "higher" and more "enlightened" white people.

Many Southern Americans saw slavery not only as acceptable and necessary for their society, but also as an institution established and sanctioned by God. During his inaugural address as provisional President of the Confederate States of America, Jefferson Davis said,

[Slavery] was established by decree of Almighty God...it is sanctioned in the Bible, in both Testaments, from Genesis to Revelation...it has existed in all ages, has been found among the people of the highest civilization, and in nations of the highest proficiency in the arts.[5]

The Reverend Alexander Campbell said, "There is not one verse in the Bible inhibiting slavery, but many regulating it. It is not then, we conclude, immoral."[6] The Reverend R. Furman, a Baptist in South Carolina, had this to say: "The right of holding slaves is clearly established in the Holy Scriptures, both by precept and example."[7]

These quotes are typical of what most Southern Americans, including many, many Christians, believed. Yes, often our "cultural lenses" taint how we read God's instruction manual. Slavery was thoroughly entrenched in Southern society and culture. Hereditary and environmental racist influences blinded them (I must now say us, as I am now a resident of a Southern state) to the gross immorality and injustice of slavery as well as to the inconsistency of a pro-slavery stance with the true message of the gospel.

In the years since the end of the Civil War, many segments of the white Church in America have perpetuated racial stereotypes and encouraged racial separation, even in church. Dr. Martin Luther King, Jr., once said that the most segregated hour in America is 11:00 on Sunday morning. Although much progress has been made, after 30 years Dr. King's statement is just as true, in many ways, as it was when he first made it.

On the surface, the American racial landscape today looks much different than it did even 50 years ago. Desegregation and equal opportunity are the laws of the land in education, housing, employment, public facilities, and virtually every other area of life, yet racial tension between blacks and whites remains. African-American church buildings have been burned to the ground. The problem actually seems to be escalating. Why? One reason is that "integration" only addresses the surface, or the appearance, of the race problem. True racial harmony cannot be achieved by any law or legislation. Racial harmony requires reconciliation of the differences that divide us, and reconciliation is a matter of the heart. It is also the ministry of the true Church. The answer to racism is found only in the liberating gospel of Jesus Christ.

ROUGH ROAD TO RECONCILIATION

The road to reconciliation will not be, is not, and never has been, an easy one. There is a lot of baggage to deal with on both sides. White American Christians have the legacy of a Church that in many ways and for many years has been an obstacle standing in the way of blacks, both by supporting slavery and by hindering blacks' full spiritual, social, and economic development.

In the earliest years of slavery, a general practice existed that discouraged evangelizing slaves in the belief that a pagan slave would be a better slave—a more controllable slave—than a Christian slave would. Some even believed that blacks were subhuman and did not have souls to save! There was also the moral dilemma of a Christian slave owner keeping a fellow Christian in bondage. As concern for the "souls" of slaves grew, evangelizing them became more accepted, but laws were passed expressly stating that a slave's conversion to Christ was not automatically grounds for setting him free. For many, this removed both the moral dilemma and the economic risk of bringing slaves to Christ.

Over the course of the years, many African-Americans, both slave and free, became authentic Christians. They were touched by God in many of the same revivals that swept through white

America: the First Great Awakening of the 1730s and '40s, the second Great Awakening of the 1790s and early 1800s, and subsequent movements. Believing slaves developed a vibrant faith with a style of worship and expression uniquely their own, and the gospel spread readily through many slave communities.

However, due to fear of slave insurrections, in most places slaves were forbidden to congregate together in any numbers, even for worship. Often slaves were taken to their master's church where they sat shackled together in specially designated pews. Many slaves defied the rules, however, and risked severe punishment to sneak off into the woods to attend secret prayer meetings and worship services with other slaves. Imagine, this is part of our "American history"!

On the other hand, many slaves rejected the "white man's religion" because they clearly saw the hypocrisy between what Christianity taught and the lifestyles and practices of the white Christians whom they knew.

As the number of African-American Christians grew, many of the traditionally "white" denominations, particularly the Methodists and Baptists, were flooded with black members. The white leadership of these denominations sought to limit black members' involvement by prohibiting them from holding any positions of leadership or authority of any kind. This helped precipitate not only separate black and white churches in the same denominations, but also the formation of completely independent, all-black denominations, thus widening the rift between black and white Christians. That rift still remains today, and it is only just now beginning to close.

But it's a two-sided street. Reconciliation is difficult also because of the accumulated hurt and anger among blacks due to generations of bigotry and injustice (not to mention the reactionary guilt and defensiveness of many whites). In *Healing America's Wounds*, John Dawson provides an excellent discussion of this.

> When a people have been oppressed and wounded and
> the yoke is lifted, when the circumstances finally

change, the emancipation of their souls is not immediate. The first generation, those who are free but carrying the memory of hurt, are often too numb to be angry....The past is literally unspeakable, and...they are reluctant to talk about it....

This means that the second generation...are often relatively ignorant of the suffering that overshadows the recent past. It is often the third generation that stumbles across the awful truth in their search for understanding about identity: the unspeakable is spoken about and anger and bitterness surface into the public domain. This also means that the grandchildren of the oppressor often face the greatest hostility and rejection from elements of the offended people group, leaving them bewildered and struggling for an appropriate response.[8]

BREAKING THE BONDS OF RACISM

One key to racial reconciliation is understanding the false premise that lies behind racism: that "races" are genetically distinct and specific and that some "races" are inherently superior to others. This is a complete and total fiction with its roots in a time long before knowledge of modern biology, propped up by generations of people who needed to justify their enslavement and persecution of people who were superficially different from them. Once again, John Dawson says it well:

Biologically, there are no races. So-called racial characteristics vary so much from individual to individual that all attempts at establishing distinct biological units that deserve classification are arbitrary. Each person has tens of thousands of different genes. At the genetic level, human beings are incredibly diverse in a way that transcends geographic dispersion. Therefore, what we call a race is a classification of culture, having more to do with tribal membership or national citizenship than any real genetic distinction.

For some reason, skin color has been the defining characteristic in cross-cultural relationships. No personal physical feature, except gender, has made such an impact on the fates of individuals and people groups, yet pigmentation is a relatively superficial thing.[9]

If there is any issue that keeps the American Church from reaching its greatest potential, it is racism. Until we resolve this problem at a heart level, we will not see the fullness of God in our midst and our ministry. As Dawson says, "If racism is the thing more than any other that reveals the spiritual poverty of the American Church, let's take up this issue as the first order of public confession."[10] I give a hearty "Amen!"

Racial reconciliation calls not only for confession of sin, but also for the courage and the willingness to enter into dialogue with one another on more than a surface level. We need to learn to talk to each other honestly and openly about the hurt and the anger, the fear and the resentment, the bitterness and the misunderstanding that divide us.

A NEW DAY IS DAWNING

Efforts are underway in many parts of the country. The Promise Keepers groups have made great strides in this direction with their ethnically diverse meetings nationwide. In some cases there have been denominational recognition of responsibility. For example, the Southern Baptist Convention, the largest Protestant denomination in America (it had split with northern Baptists in 1845 over the slavery issue), has in recent years adopted several resolutions at its annual meetings expressing regret and apology for racist policies and practices of the past.

Today I live in Franklin, Tennessee—site of one of the bloodiest battles in the "Uncivil War." Redemptively, a ministry called Empty Hands Fellowship is doing a great work of reconciliation in this quaint community. The leadership is comprised of one African-American and one European-American pastor who truly love one another. What a joy it was in September 2002 to witness, at the town square in Franklin, a public rally of praise, prayer and testimony of black and white leaders embracing one another in Christ.

I believe an amazing work of grace is taking place in our nation today. In many metropolitan cities, the fastest growing and largest congregations are African-American. I believe this is the work of a just God, who knows the pain of years and is returning dignity and honor to these previously enslaved people. Yes, a new day is upon us.

We could tear other pages out of history and consider issues concerning the Chinese, Irish, Polish, Japanese, and many other nationalities. But to heal America's wounds, we must begin at one of our greatest historic sins and stains—the fear, prejudice, and pride between white and black Christians. The hideous shadow of slavery and its legacy of racial hostility and violence must be banished from the land.

AN HONEST CONFESSION

As a white European Christian, I ask my African-American brothers and sisters to forgive us for denying to you the love of Christ we claimed for ourselves and shared among ourselves. Forgive us for our blindness, our prejudice, and our spiritual arrogance. We confess our contempt of your culture, your identity, and your personhood. Forgive us for so often denying your essential worth in the eyes of God and man. Forgive us, my friends! We need you!

We have sinned, God. Forgive us, Your Caucasian children, for our bigotry and injustice toward our brothers and sisters of African descent—people created in Your image and likeness and precious in Your sight. Cleanse us from our arrogance and for our pride of place, our pride of face, our pride of grace, and our pride of race. Cleanse our hearts of any trace of prejudice and renew a right spirit within us.

May new beginnings emerge out of the ashes of racism. Lord, lead us boldly into reconciliation and unity with all believers, so that we may, as Your Bride, be prepared for Your coming— pure and spotless, holy and innocent, and undivided in our love. I proclaim that the African-American community will have a revival movement that will surpass the days of William Seymour and the Azuza Street Revival. May it ever be so!

◆

REFLECTION QUESTIONS

1. What motivated the European settlers in North America to enslave the African peoples?
2. What does the word *prejudice* mean to you and what fuels it, in your opinion?
3. What was one of the great historic atrocities done in the United States that you could confess before the throne in Jesus' name?

RECOMMENDED READING

The Three Prejudices by Kelley Varner (Destiny Image, 1997)
Right or Reconciled? by Joseph Garlington (Destiny Image, 1998)
Free at Last? The Reality of Racism in the Church by Michael Goings (Treasure House, 1995)

ENDNOTES

1. Michael E. Goings, *Free at Last? The Reality of Racism in the Church* (Shippensburg, PA: Treasure House, 1995), 10.

2. Goings, *Free at Last?*, 5.

3. Kelley Varner, *The Three Prejudices* (Shippensburg, PA: Destiny Image Publishers, 1997), 110-111.

4. Goings, *Free at Last?*, 6-10.

5. Quoted in "What the Bible says about Slavery." 10 Sept. 1999. www.religioustolerance.org/sla_bibl.htm>.

6. Quoted in "What the Bible says about Slavery."

7. Quoted in "What the Bible says about Slavery."

8. John Dawson, *Healing America's Wounds* (Ventura, CA: Regal Books, 1994), 184-185.

9. Dawson, *Healing America's Wounds*, 205.

10. Dawson, *Healing America's Wounds*, 209.

Chapter 9

CLEANSING THE HOUSE
OF GREED AND IDOLATRY

Jesus is coming to cleanse His Father's house! Watch out—
a lot of tables might get turned over in the process. One of
the very first prophetic words I ever heard pop out of my mouth
some 30 years ago stated this was exactly what He was intending
to do. "As it was in the last week of Jesus' earthly ministry in the
flesh, so it will be in the last week of the 'last days' of His ministry by the Spirit in the earth—He will come to cleanse His Father's House." I am personally convinced that the Holy Spirit
will do a clean sweep of the sins of greed and idolatry as a part
of this great end-time move of God.

This work of sanctification will hit the Church in the nation
but will not stop until reformation and restoration come to the
nation itself. God has a big plan in store. The Holy Spirit will
manifest Himself as the "white tornado of God," creating a swirl
of activity that leaves nothing in its sight untouched. Watch out,
world—here He comes!

LOOKING BELOW THE SURFACE

There can be little doubt that the United States of America is
one of the most blessed nations in all history. Certainly God's
hand was behind the establishment of a nation that has demonstrated before the world a level of personal, national, and religious liberty never before achieved. For more than 200 years this
country truly has been a beacon of freedom shining in the eyes of
oppressed peoples everywhere. Millions the world over who
have desired a better life for themselves and their children have

sought to come to these shores to fulfill their dreams. Missionary zeal and a hunger for religious freedom fired the hearts of many of the earliest settlers of this land.

Historically, we are the most prosperous nation of all time. On the surface everything looks fine. But just as in the same manner in which some people clean their houses—quickly sweeping the dirt under the rug to make things look fine on the surface—things are not always as they seem. All is not well after all. A closer look reveals cracks in the polished veneer of our well-being.

Lurking just below the surface is a society in the grip of rapacious greed, all-consuming selfishness, shallow materialism, empty humanism, and for many, grinding poverty. Millions of Americans observe a "practical atheism"—giving only lip service to God. Respect for sanctity of life has given way to debates on "quality" of life while the perceived worth of the aged and the infirm, the mentally deficient, and the unborn has been degraded. Even in view of 9/11/01 and the collapse of the Twin Towers, our nation only turned "towards" God but in reality not "to" God. Clearly, something is terribly wrong.

Whatever happened to honor, honesty, integrity, morality, ethics, and character? They have been sacrificed on the altar of ambition, greed, lust, indulgence, hedonism, political expediency, and personal convenience. Quite frankly, America has a love affair with mammon. We worship at his altar, commit our lives to the pursuit of his values, and seek to build our society and culture according to his standards. As a nation we have sold our souls to this hedonistic spirit.

No Man Can Serve Two Masters

Judging from the four Gospels, we infer that during His earthly ministry Jesus had more to say about money, our use of it, and our attitude toward it than about any other single subject. The attention Jesus gave to this subject indicates both the power of its appeal to human consciousness and the potential danger of that appeal. Nowhere is this seen more clearly than in Jesus' encounter with the rich young ruler (see Mt. 19:16-22).

What Jesus is saying here is that we cannot have divided loyalties. Either we serve God or we serve mammon; we cannot do both. We tend to think of the word *mammon* as simply a synonym for wealth or money. In reality, the truth goes much deeper. Mammon is a word of Chaldean origin that came to mean "wealth personified" or "avarice deified."[1] In other words, mammon is greed or covetousness elevated to the status of a god. This is not merely an abstract concept, however; there is a principality involved here. As Dr. C. Peter Wagner writes,

> Covetousness is allegiance to a false god named Mammon. *Mamona* is an Aramaic term for wealth. First century rabbis considered *Mamona* a demonic being and a rival of God. That is why the NIV translated Jesus' words in Luke 16:13: "You cannot serve both God and Money [Mammon]." It is correct to capitalize "Money" or "Mammon" because it is a proper name. Mammon is a person, not a thing or an urge or an attitude....When Jesus mentioned Mammon, it was in the context of not being able to serve two masters. Serving any supernatural master in the demonic world, like Mammon, is hard-core idolatry.[2]

Hard-core idolatry? In America? It is the tragic truth. Our national obsession with mammon—the accumulation of wealth and the pursuit of pleasure and plenty—as the driving force of our lives reveals that idolatry is deeply embedded in our society. The damning indictment that we must face is this: The United States of America is an idolatrous nation!

No Other Gods?

Throughout His Word, God has made His feelings about idolatry perfectly clear: He hates it! The first two commandments deal specifically with the subject, and their placement at the head of the list indicates that they are fundamental—they are foundational for everything that follows.

> *You shall have no other gods before Me. You shall not make for yourself an idol, or any likeness of what is in heaven above*

or on the earth beneath or in the water under the earth. You
shall not worship them or serve them; for I, the Lord your
God, am a jealous God....(Exodus 20:3-5).

God will have no rivals. His prohibition of idolatry is straightforward; there are to be no carved images of celestial bodies or supernatural beings (heaven above), land creatures (the earth beneath), or sea creatures (the water under the earth). That covers the entire created realm, both natural and supernatural. God alone is to be worshiped and served.

Biblically speaking, idolatry refers to the actual worship of someone or something other than God. In his excellent booklet *Hard-Core Idolatry*, Dr. C. Peter Wagner writes,

Idolatry is worshiping, serving, pledging allegiance to, doing acts of obeisance to, paying homage to, forming alliances with, making covenants with, seeking power from, or in any other way exalting any supernatural being other than God. The supernatural beings refer to angels, cherubim, seraphim, Satan, principalities, powers, deities, territorial spirits, goddesses, and demonic beings on any other level.[3]

Dr. Wagner further adds,

[Idolatry] is about worshiping beings in the invisible world, which often leads to a special recognition of tangible objects ("carved images" or idols), in the visible world. What you see in the visible world is a person bowing down or making a sacrifice or burning incense either to an image of some kind or to a feature of creation like the sun, a mountain, a rock, or a river. What is actually taking place behind the scenes is a spiritual transaction with one or more spirit beings in the invisible world. This is what I am calling hard-core idolatry.[4]

Many believers would be quick to point out that there is no power in an inert image of wood or stone. That's true enough. So what's the danger? The danger lies not in the image or idol itself, but in the demonic spirit that it represents.

According to Paul, then, idolatry is worshiping, sacrificing to, or serving a demonic being. America's allegiance to Mammon certainly falls into this category. Consider a society in which one teenager kills another teenager for his two-hundred-dollar pair of sneakers; or where the weak and powerless are routinely trod upon, abused, and dispossessed by the more fortunate in their endless striving for more, more, more.

A BLOODTHIRSTY "GOD"

Worship of mammon is not the only form of idolatry in the land. There is another that is even more hideous; it is a new, modern manifestation of an age-old blood cult. Idolatry involves the worship of demons. The Old Testament is full of references to idolatry, but it contains only four clear-cut references to demons.[5] Each of these four refer to idolatrous practices in Israel and occur in the context of making sacrifices to demons, which involves the shedding of innocent blood. It is the shedding of blood that empowers the demonic forces behind the idols. In some cases children were the innocent victims:

> [They] served their idols, which became a snare to them. They even sacrificed their sons and their daughters to the demons, and shed innocent blood, the blood of their sons and their daughters, whom they sacrificed to the idols of Canaan; and the land was polluted with the blood (Psalm 106:36-38).

The Old Testament also contains eight references to Molech, a false deity (demon) identified as the "god" of the Ammonites.[6] He was a grim and bloodthirsty principality whose worship rituals apparently involved human sacrifice, particularly of children. First Kings 11:7b describes Molech as "the detestable idol of the sons of Ammon." Apparently there were some within the nation of Israel who served Molech. "They built the high places of Baal that are in the valley of Ben-hinnom to cause their sons and their daughters to pass through the fire to Molech, which I had not commanded them nor had it entered My mind that they should do this abomination, to cause Judah to sin" (Jer. 32:35).

"To pass through the fire" is the reference to human sacrifice to Molech, although the exact process is not clear. According to some rabbinic writers, a bronze statue in the form of a man but with the head of an ox was used. Children were placed inside the statue, which was then heated from below. Loud, pounding drums drowned out the cries and screams of the children.[7] No wonder such a twisted "worship" practice would be an "abomination" to God! Innocent children by the thousands were sacrificed horribly to sate the blood lust of a demonic "god."

The bloodthirsty "spirit of Molech" has been alive in every age, including our own, in various adapted forms. In the "civilized" Western world of today, it is the driving force behind the burgeoning abortion industry. Because of the U.S. Supreme Court decision in *Roe v. Wade* in 1973, the United States now has the most liberal abortion laws of any nation in the world. Since that infamous ruling 30 years ago, an estimated *40 million* unborn children have been killed in the womb. This equates to *4,000 abortions a day or one every 24 seconds!*[8] These figures are for the United States alone; they do not include abortions performed in other countries.

According to abortion statistical studies as recent as 1995, there is additional startling news. The abortion rate is virtually the same among Protestant young women in the United States as it is among non-churched women.[9] Something is terribly wrong here! The sin is as great in the Church as it is in the world! *Father, have mercy on us Your people!*

Were these 40 million abortions "medically necessary"? Hardly. To listen to the pro-choice people you would think that abortion is a "right" that is absolutely essential to the physical health of women. Abortion is "justified" to preserve the life of the mother, to prevent a "defective" child, or in cases of rape or incest. According to Dr. C. Everett Koop, former U.S. Surgeon General, this is a fallacious argument. "Even if these were valid reasons, they would account for only 2 percent of all abortions. A full 98 percent of abortions occur for reasons of convenience and economy."[10]

"Convenience and economy"? What's wrong with us? Since 1973, 40 million unborn babies have been sacrificed at the bloody altar of Molech for reasons inspired by the spirit of mammon! It is a "holocaust" that, in numbers alone, dwarfs that of the Nazi genocide of Jews and other "undesirables" in the 1930s and '40s. There is no way under the sun to justify such deliberate termination of human life at any level, much less the all but incomprehensible scale occurring in our country. Dr. James Dobson of Focus on the Family expressed it well when he wrote,

> No rationalization can justify detaching a healthy little human being from its place of safety and leaving him or her to suffocate on a porcelain table. No social or financial considerations can assuage our collective guilt for destroying lives which were being fashioned in the image of God Himself. Throughout the Gospels, Jesus revealed a tenderness toward boys and girls ("Suffer the little children to come unto Me"), and some of His most frightening warnings were addressed to those who would hurt them. How can He hold us blameless for our wanton feticide and infanticide? As the Lord said to Cain, who had killed Abel, "Your brother's blood calls to me from the ground!" (Genesis 4:10)[11]

As a nation, our sins are great. Yet I believe that some of America's greatest destiny awaits us. But we must remove the blockades so that the promise can yet come forth. We have sinned as a Church! We have sinned as a nation!

Pure and Undefiled Religion

At the heart of God-pleasing faith is a concern and compassion for the poor and oppressed. This is not because such a concern earns God's favor, but because it is a reflection of God's heart, and only those who know God can reflect His heart. Compassion for the poor is a natural outgrowth of "saving faith," one fruit of a redeemed life. James, the brother of our Lord, expressed it this way: "Pure and undefiled religion in the sight of our God and Father is this: to visit orphans and widows in their distress, and to keep oneself unstained by the world" (Jas. 1:27).

"Orphans and widows" represented the lowest strata of society, the poorest of the poor. They are without power or influence, without anyone to plead their cause, and with usually little
opportunity to better their situation. God's people are called to
minister to just such as these. We receive our marching orders
from Christ, whom, "He has anointed Me to preach good news to
the poor" (Lk. 4:18a NIV). Throughout His ministry Jesus identified with the poor and dispossessed of society. His identification
was so complete that He said that to provide for or to deny "the
least of these" was to provide for or to deny Him (Mt. 25:40,45).

If there is anything that the Bible makes clear, it is God's
heart for the poor.

- *God cares for the poor.*

"If there is a poor man with you, one of your brothers...you
shall not harden your heart, nor close your hand from your
poor brother; but you shall freely open your hand to him,
and shall generously lend him sufficient for his need in
whatever he lacks" (Deut. 15:7-8).

- *God defends the poor.*

"Who executes justice for the oppressed; who gives food to
the hungry. The Lord sets the prisoners free. The Lord opens
the eyes of the blind; the Lord raises up those who are
bowed down; the Lord loves the righteous; the Lord protects
the strangers; He supports the fatherless and the widow, but
He thwarts the way of the wicked" (Ps. 146:7-9).

- *God loves the poor.*

"He who oppresses the poor taunts his Maker, but he who is
gracious to the needy honors Him" (Prov. 14:31).

- *God judges those who close their hearts and ears to the poor.*

"Therefore because you impose heavy rent on the poor and
exact a tribute of grain from them, though you have built
houses of well-hewn stone, yet you will not live in them;
you have planted pleasant vineyards, yet you will not drink
their wine. For I know your transgressions are many and
your sins are great, you who distress the righteous and accept
bribes, and turn aside the poor in the gate" (Amos 5:11-12).

CULTIVATING GOD'S HEART FOR THE POOR

Before the American Church can be truly effective in dealing with the idolatry in our land and in cultivating God's heart for the poor, we must acknowledge and confess that we have been part of the problem. Idolatry in the Church? Yes! Our tendency in North America is to model a kind of demanding, self-centered "gospel" that is nothing other than the spirit of mammon with a foothold in the Church.

Many of the major problems in the United States can be linked to the fact that, as a nation, we have generally neglected and abused our poor. In our covetousness and greed, in our drive for personal comfort and convenience, in our daily fight to "get ours" and to "look out for number one," we have no room in our hearts for the poor. They are an inconvenience, an embarrassing reminder that all is not well in the heartland. We do not have God's eyes or God's heart for the poor. O Lord, take the blinders off our hearts and minds, for Jesus' sake, I pray.

In his book *Liberating the Church*, Howard Snyder addresses the challenge that the Church faces in reaching out to the poor. He states that the Church must both work for the poor and be of the poor, in the sense of making the poor its "special concern in evangelism, justice ministries and way of life."[12] Snyder then identifies four things the Church must do to reach the poor:[13]

- *The Church must identify with and learn from the poor.*

This involves learning to see life from the point of view of the poor, learning to identify with God's point of view toward the poor, and learning to deal with our prejudice against the poor.

- *The Church must defend the cause of the poor.*

We can do this in two ways. First, we can work to provide relief for the poor and help them improve their own lives; secondly, we can examine our own lifestyles in order to be more responsible in the way we live.

- *The Church must offer Christ to the poor.*

The poor need the gospel as much as anyone else does, and "offering Christ to the poor can be done with integrity only by those who take the side of the poor and learn from them."

• *The Church must be a reconciled and reconciling community of and with the poor.*

As the Church identifies with and works among the poor, defending their cause and presenting Christ to them, the basis is laid for the Christian revolution. We are not to be the Church of the poor against the rich and middle class, but the Church of all peoples standing on the side of the oppressed.

DESTROYING OUR IDOLS

Over the past six chapters I have talked about specific generational and historic sins that we as Christians need to address in our land: the clergy-laity separation; the gender gap; the need for reconciliation with Jews, the First Nations People (Native Americans), and African-Americans; and the problems of greed and idolatry. This is by no means a comprehensive list of the obstacles and barriers that stand in the way of spiritual awakening and revival in our land; they only represent the major issues that the Holy Spirit has laid on my heart to address.

Of the six issues discussed, I placed the greed and idolatry problem last because it is the most subtle and critical. Until we take seriously the problem of idolatry in America and deal with it in a biblical manner, we will not see full awakening and revival come. Much insight has been gained in recent years and much high-level strategic spiritual warfare has taken place with a heart to reclaim the cities of our land for God. Unless we deal with the idolatry problem, though, we will see little real lasting success.

Dr. C. Peter Wagner makes this very clear:

The finest of our leaders may competently apply all the excellent insights that God has given us for city transformation over the last few years on the highest levels in our cities, but if we do not also deal a significant and simultaneous blow to idolatry, we will not see our dream for city transformation come true.[14]

My brothers and sisters, the day is almost spent. It's time to take a stand! The Lord is looking for those who will stand in the gap before Him for the land, that He not destroy it (see Ezek. 22:30). We need to cleanse our own hearts first and then stand in the gap for our families, our friends, our neighbors, our schools, our cities, and our nation. Let's take a stand together for God's light to shine by confessing our historic sins. Only then will we remove satan's legal basis to blind us.

Dear Lord, forgive us! Forgive us for the greed, for the covetousness that runs rampant in our land! Forgive us as a nation for squandering Your blessings and for turning from Your high call to serve the spirit of mammon! Forgive us for our monstrous holocaust of unborn children—created in Your image and precious in Your sight—sacrificed in the spirit of Molech for the sake of greed and convenience! Forgive us for neglecting the poor and needy around us, for despising their dignity and demeaning their worth. Forgive us for not displaying Your heart for the poor.

Lord, help us to strip away the idols in our heart and in our national consciousness. Give us Your heart for the poor—a heart of love, compassion, and mercy. Instead of abortion on demand, may the greatest youth revival in all of history begin. Instead of consumer greed, may a mighty missions movement spring forth suddenly. I proclaim restoration to our inner cities and safety to every child in its mother's womb. Father, let Your glory fill our land! May the best be yet to come.

REFLECTION QUESTIONS

1. Give a definition for "hard-core idolatry."
2. How do you see the sins of idolatry and greed to be connected?
3. What are the demonic spirits behind the abortion industry in America?

RECOMMENDED READING

Hard-Core Idolatry by C. Peter Wagner (Wagner Leadership Institute, 1999)

When You Were Formed in Secret by Gary Bergel (pamphlet by Intercessors for America, 1980, 1998)

ENDNOTES

1. James Strong, *Strong's Exhaustive Concordance of the Bible* (Peabody, MA: Hendrickson Publishers, n.d.), *mammon*, #G3126.

2. C. Peter Wagner, *Hard-Core Idolatry: Facing the Facts* (Colorado Springs, CO: Wagner Leadership Institute, 1998), 17.

3. Wagner, *Hard-Core Idolatry*, 11-12.

4. Wagner, *Hard-Core Idolatry*, 12.

5. These are Leviticus 17:7; Deuteronomy 32:17; Second Chronicles 11:15; and Psalm 106:36-38. Of course, this does not include references to satan in the Book of Job or to lucifer in Isaiah 14:12 (KJV only).

6. These are Leviticus 18:21; 20:2-5; First Kings 11:7; Second Kings 23:10; and Jeremiah 32:35.

7. Paul E. Robertson, "Molech," *Holman Bible Dictionary* (Nashville, TN: Holman Bible Publishers, 1991). *QuickVerse 4.0 Deluxe Bible Reference Collection*. CD-ROM. Parsons Technology, 1992-1996.

8. Gary Bergel, *Abortion in America* (Leesburg, VA: Intercessors for America, 1998), II-4.

9. This statistical information was posted by Intercessors for America from the original Henshaw/Kost Abortion Patients survey done in 1994-1995.

10. C. Everett Koop, "...at the Crossroads," in Bergel, *Abortion in America*, II-7.

11. James C. Dobson, "Abortion & the Future..." in Bergel, *Abortion in America*, II-7.

12. Snyder, *Liberating the Church*, 240.

13. Snyder, *Liberating the Church*, 241-245.

14. Wagner, *Hard-Core Idolatry*, 34.

Section Three

FIRE!
HITTING OUR INTERCESSORY MARK

Chapter 10

Enforcing the Victory of Calvary

E ver go hunting? There are three basic steps: Ready, aim, fire! You might need to clean out your gun before you attempt to fire it again. After you clean and oil your gun, you next take aim. This is where you set your sights with a careful, proper, steady gaze. Your focus must be clear and your aim steady toward the desired target. Then, finally, after preparing your weapon and taking aim, you pull the trigger and *fire*!

In the first section of this book, we emphasized "getting ready" by laying a proper foundation of representational repentance and the power of proclamation. In the middle portion, we set our prayerful "aim" on historical targets for social and spiritual change. This last section will cast light on "firing" this weapon of spiritual warfare called intercession. So let's round the corner now and consider how we can fervently and effectively "enforce the victory" that is already ours.

The Greatest Event in History

The greatest event in all of history began in the humblest of circumstances, completely insignificant in the eyes of men. A baby boy was born to a simple peasant girl, perhaps no more than 14 or 15 years old, who had taken shelter with her carpenter husband in a cave used for keeping and feeding livestock. The child grew up in obscurity and at the age of 30 embarked on a brief three-year career as an itinerant preacher and teacher. During His entire life He never traveled farther than two hundred miles from His birthplace. He attracted a small group of followers, taught about the Kingdom of God, healed people, and cast out demons. His unorthodox style quickly ran afoul of the religious authorities, however, and eventually He was betrayed by one of His own followers.

Branded a heretic and a blasphemer, He died a humiliating and excruciatingly painful death, being nailed to a rude and rough cross as an enemy of the state. After His death, He was buried in a borrowed tomb and His small band of followers scattered in fear and grief. It was over. So ended the brief and seemingly tragically failed life of Jesus, the carpenter from Nazareth, now consigned to the dustbin of history. He left no statues or monuments to His memory; no written record of His life, deeds, or teachings to live on after Him; and no children to carry on His name. Or so it seemed.

By the worldly standards of man, Jesus' life was an utter failure. But from God's perspective, the life of Jesus was perfectly fulfilled and gloriously victorious. His monuments are the cross and the empty tomb. The record of His life, deeds, and teachings is the New Testament, penned by His disciples, who were inspired by the Holy Spirit.

The death and resurrection of Jesus Christ were the greatest events in history. Nothing else has so affected the destiny and future of mankind. According to John 1:18b, Jesus is "the only begotten God, who is in the bosom of the Father." This means that Jesus was the very heart of God Himself. There was a moment in history where the Father in eternity placed His hand into His bosom and flung His Son forth into the world of time and space, declaring, "Here is the very best I can give: the love of My own heart."

That love, the very Word of the Father, was crucified between two thieves. There it pleased God to throw upon His Son all the sin, wickedness, and corruption of every generation, race, and nation of mankind—past, present, and future. Jesus Christ was "the Lamb of God who takes away the sin of the world" (Jn. 1:29b). The sinless One became sin for us, and the penalty of our judgment fell upon Him. His blood washed away our sin, and His righteousness was imputed to us. The barrier of sin separating us from God was removed through the most demonstrative and extravagant act of love in all of history.

At the darkest moment of all, when it seemed as though all was lost, Jesus cried out in triumph, "It is finished!" (Jn. 19:30) Jesus died a gruesome death. But then He rose from the dead three days later, as sin and death stayed in the grave, conquered forever. Jesus' resurrection sealed the victory won at the cross.

The greatest act in history is also the grandest promise in Scripture: "For God so loved the world, that He gave His only begotten Son, that whoever believes in Him shall not perish, but have eternal life" (Jn. 3:16).

THE IMPORTANCE OF THE SHED BLOOD

It is the shed blood of Jesus that makes atonement for our sins. Why is the blood so important? Blood represents the life force of all flesh. It is essential for life. According to Scripture, life is in the blood (see Lev. 17:11).

Blood is also essential for the forgiveness of sin. "And according to the Law, one may almost say, all things are cleansed with blood, and without shedding of blood there is no forgiveness" (Heb. 9:22). The penalty for sin is death. Atonement, or the forgiveness of sin, requires the blood of an innocent whose death is accepted in place of the guilty. This is what was symbolized in the nation of Israel by the lamb sacrifices that were performed daily. These sacrifices pointed to the ultimate sacrifice of the Lamb of God, Jesus Christ.

The Jewish priests ministered the sacrifices daily in the outer tabernacle. Only once a year, on the Day of Atonement, did the high priest—and he alone—enter the Holy of Holies to make atonement for himself and the people. He never entered the Holy of Holies, the Most Holy Place, without the blood of the sacrifice. To do otherwise would mean his death. The Holy of Holies represented the very presence of God Himself. There was no access to the Presence without the shedding of sacrificial blood.

According to the law, after the high priest had ministered at the altar of incense on this day, he would go beyond the veil into the Most Holy Place. There he would take first the blood of the bull and then the blood of the goat and sprinkle it with his finger on the mercy seat and in front of the mercy seat, seven times each. Then, going back outside the veil, he sprinkled blood on the horns of the altar, again seven times (see Lev. 16:11-19).

Why seven times? A closer look at these verses in Leviticus reveals some very interesting things. The blood was sprinkled in three distinct locations seven times each. Some Bible scholars have indicated that the number three represents the Trinity, or the fullness of the Godhead, and that the number seven is the number of completion and perfection. The sprinkling of the blood seven times in three places is then a picture of what was to come in Jesus Christ.

When Jesus, our High Priest, shed His blood, He did a complete and perfect work! It was finished. The work of atonement was accomplished perfectly through the blood of this one man—the second Adam, the Lamb of God, Jesus Christ the Lord!

SEVEN WAYS CHRIST'S BLOOD WAS SHED

There is another way that the blood of Jesus parallels the sprinkling of the blood seven times by the high priest. We can identify in the Scriptures seven specific ways that Jesus' blood was shed.

1. "And being in agony He was praying very fervently; and His sweat became like drops of blood, falling down upon the ground" (Lk. 22:44).

Jesus was praying in Gethsemane the night before He died. In the intensity of the moment and from the anguish of His soul as He chose His Father's cup and not His own, as He willed Himself to identify with the sins of the world, blood began to flow from His pores along with His sweat. At that moment Jesus was in the place of mighty wrestling and travail of soul.

The cross in our lives is the place where God's will and our will cross. Actually following God is often easier than making the decision to follow in the first place. This is where Jesus struggled; He knew what lay ahead. By yielding Himself to His Father here, Jesus won the battle in advance. He left Gethsemane and faced the cross with calmness, confidence, and peace. The blood was "sprinkled"—once.

2. "Then they spat in His face and beat Him with their fists; and others slapped Him, and said, 'Prophesy to us, You Christ; who is the one who hit You?' " (Mt. 26:67-68)

Jesus was standing before the high priest and the San-hedrin, the Jewish high council. In response to the high priest's direct question, Jesus acknowledged that He was the Son of God. Enraged at this "blasphemy," the priests and council members vented their hatred for God's Holy One with their fists. The prophet Micah records a comparable passage: "With a rod they will smite the judge of Israel on the cheek" (Mic. 5:1b). Blood from this beating began to flow down the face of Jesus. The blood was "sprinkled"—twice.

3. "I gave My back to those who strike Me, and My cheeks to those who pluck out the beard; I did not cover My face from humiliation and spitting" (Is. 50:6).

Although the plucking out of the beard is not specifically recorded in the Gospel accounts of Jesus' suffering, it is a part of Isaiah's prophetic description of the Messiah's travail. Imagine for a moment the torturous pain of having the hair literally ripped off your face! As a man, I cannot begin to imagine the agony and pain of someone forcefully pulling out my beard! No doubt when this was done to Jesus, patches of flesh were torn off as well. Now there was more than blood oozing from His pores and trickling from the bruises and gashes on His face; it flowed freely from open wounds of raw flesh. The blood was "sprinkled"—three times.

4. "Then he released Barabbas for them; but after having Jesus scourged, he handed Him over to be crucified" (Mt. 27:26).

Even though he knew Jesus was innocent of any wrong-doing, Pilate bowed to the pressure of the Jewish leaders and or-dered Jesus scourged. Psalm 129:3 gives a good description: "The plowers plowed upon my back; they lengthened their furrows." The Roman scourge was a whip with multiple leather strips, each fitted with metal balls and sharp pieces of bone designed to rip flesh from the body with every lash. Like a plow opens furrows in a field, the scourging laid open Jesus' back, probably down to the raw bone in places. The blood was "sprinkled"—four times.

5. "And after twisting together a crown of thorns, they put it on His head, and a reed in His right hand; and they knelt down before Him and mocked Him, saying, 'Hail, King of the Jews!' " (Mt. 27:29)

These were not merely short, small thorns such as those on a prickly rosebush. They were probably several inches long and forcefully jammed down on Jesus' head. Some scholars believe that the word *crown* here may refer in fact to a "cap" of sorts. If this is true, then the thorns covered Jesus' head, and every one of them drew blood. The blood was "sprinkled"—five times.

6. "And when they had crucified Him, they divided up His garments among themselves by casting lots" (Mt. 27:35).

Nails were driven through Jesus' hands and feet into the rough wooden cross. He hung with His arms at such an angle that it cut off His breathing and nearly dislocated His shoulders. The only way He could breathe was to push Himself upright against the nails. Blood poured from His nail wounds. Thus the blood was "sprinkled"—six times.

7. "One of the soldiers pierced His side with a spear, and immediately blood and water came out" (Jn. 19:34).

Jesus had already been crucified and now was completely dead. In a final indignity, a Roman soldier stabbed his spear into Jesus' side, and blood and water poured forth. The blood had now been "sprinkled"—the seventh and final time.

SEVEN WAYS CHRIST'S BLOOD AVAILS FOR US

One of the ways we overcome as believers is by declaring what the blood of Jesus has done for us. "And they [believers] overcame him [the accuser of the brethren] because of the blood of the Lamb and because of the word of their testimony, and they did not love their life even when faced with death" (Rev. 12:11). What exactly has the blood of Jesus done for us? How has His blood availed for us? Scripture reveals at least seven benefits that the shed blood of Christ gives to us.

I briefly addressed this important issue in the book my wife and I coauthored, *Encounters With a Supernatural God*. Let me give you these seven great bullets for you to fire in your spiritual warfare arsenal.[1]

1. You have been forgiven through the *blood of Jesus* (see Heb. 9:22).

2. The *blood of Jesus* has cleansed you from all sin (see 1 Jn. 1:7).

3. You have been redeemed by the *blood of the Lamb* (see Eph. 1:7).

4. By *His blood*, you are justified ["just as if"] you have never sinned (see Rom. 5:9).

5. You have been sanctified [set apart] through *Jesus' blood* for a holy calling (see Heb. 13:12).

6. Peace has been made for you *through the blood of the cross* (see Col. 1:20).

7. You now have confidence to enter the Most Holy Place by the *blood of Jesus* (see Heb. 10:19).

The blood of Christ intercedes for us! Christ Himself is ever before the Father as our Mediator. "Christ Jesus is He who died, yes, rather who was raised, who is at the right hand of God, who also intercedes for us" (Rom. 8:34b). The highest and greatest intercession of all is the blood of Jesus that speaks before the Father's throne!

Yes, Christ's blood has given us life! Through Christ's blood we receive eternal life. The breath of life that God breathed into the first Adam has been restored to Adam's fallen children through the blood of the second Adam, Jesus Christ (see 1 Cor. 15:45). We now have God's breath, God's life, in our lungs. Breathe it in—and breathe it back out on others!

PLEADING THE BLOOD

Praise God! We who are born-again believers in the Lord Jesus Christ have been covered by the blood of the Lamb! To some of you that may sound like a bunch of religious jargon, but it's not. We have been purchased by the precious blood of Jesus, the Messiah, the Son of God, our Lord. Joyfully we can proclaim with the hosts in Heaven, "Worthy are You...for You were slain, and purchased for God with Your blood men from every tribe and tongue and people and nation" (Rev. 5:9b).

He who bought us with His blood now owns us and has complete rights to us. He also has promised to protect and care for us. Just as the lamb's blood on the lintels and doorposts of the Hebrews in Egypt protected them from the scourge of the death angel, so the blood of Jesus protects us. But how do we apply the blood today so that judgment, wrath, pestilence, and disease will pass over us? We do it by pleading the blood.

There is no greater plea, no more prevailing argument to bring before God, than the suffering and atoning death of His Son. In his powerful book *Mighty Prevailing Prayer*, author Wesley Duewel wrote:

> Plead the blood. Pray till you have the assurance of God's will. Pray till you have been given by the Spirit a vision of what God longs to do, needs to do, waits to do. Pray till you are gripped by the authority of the name of Jesus. Then plead the blood of Jesus. The name of Jesus and the blood of Jesus—glory in them, stake your all on them, and use them to the glory of God and the routing of Satan.
>
> Bring before the Father the wounds of Jesus; remind the Father of the agony of Gethsemane; recall to the Father the strong cries of the Son of God as He prevailed for our world and for our salvation. Remind the Father of earth's darkest hour on Calvary, as the Son triumphed alone for you and me. Shout to heaven again Christ's triumphant call, "It is finished!" Plead the cross. Plead the blood. Plead them over and over again.[2]

That's how to prevail in effective intercession!

The great nineteenth-century English preacher Charles Spurgeon wrote that the blood of Jesus "unlocks the treasury of heaven. Many keys fit many locks, but the master key is the blood and the name of Him that died and rose again, and ever lives in heaven to save unto the uttermost."[3]

ONE DROP OF THE BLOOD OF JESUS

When my friend Mahesh Chavda ministered in the African nation of Zaire, he found himself standing in front of more than one hundred thousand people. The Holy Spirit told him to hold a mass deliverance service the next day. Mahesh said to God, "Lord, I am here alone. Where are my helpers?" To that the Lord responded, "I am your helper. Remember, one drop of the blood of My Son, Jesus, is more powerful than all the kingdom of darkness!"[4]

If we want to see generational curses lifted and sins forgiven; if we want to see true revival come to the land; if we want to prevail in intercession and see God's glory fill the earth, then we need to plead the blood. We must testify to what the blood of Jesus has accomplished for us. Plead the blood of our glorious Lord and King who died and rose again! Plead, proclaim, recite, declare, and put your trust in the work of His shed blood. This is the Bible way of "enforcing the victory of Calvary!" There is nothing like the blood of Jesus! The old gospel hymn says it so well:

> Would you be free
> From your burden of sin?
> There's power in the blood,
> Power in the blood;
> Would you o'er evil a victory win?
> There's wonderful power in the blood.
>
> Would you be whiter,
> Much whiter than snow?
> There's power in the blood,
> Power in the blood;
> Sin stains are lost
> In its lifegiving flow;
> There's wonderful power in the blood.
>
> There is power, power,
> Wonder-working power,
> In the blood of the Lamb;

There is power, power,
Wonder-working power,
In the precious blood of the Lamb.[5]

APPLY THE BLOOD: A PRAYER OF CLEANSING

Since we have been talking about pleading and applying the blood of Jesus, I want to close with a prayer to help you personally enforce the victory of Christ's cross in your own life.

Father, we cleanse our hands with the blood of Jesus. We apply the blood of Jesus to our eyes, Lord, so that we might see into the spirit realm clearly and with clarity. We apply the blood of Jesus to our ears, to cleanse our ears of any defilement, wickedness, garbage, gossip or slander that have been poured into our ears, so that we might hear clearly what You are speaking to us. We apply the blood of Jesus to our lips and to our tongue, so that You would be able to cleanse us of all those things that we have spoken that really haven't been of You at all. Father, we apply the blood of Jesus to our heart and our minds. So Father, we ask You to put the blood of Jesus on our hearts, our thoughts, and our emotions and to cleanse our minds from the dead works so that we might serve the living God.

Father, we apply the blood of Jesus to our feet. Cleanse us from the corruption in this world and from the dust of the world. Father, cleanse us of those places that we've walked in that really haven't been ordered of You. Lord, we receive the words of the Bible that say, "The steps of a righteous man are ordered by the Lord." We will have holy steps, walking on that highway of holiness. Praise You, Lord! And we ask that You cleanse us from the top of our head to the souls of our feet. Thank You, Lord!

How do we enforce the victory of Calvary? What has the power to break generational sin? Where does the power to break demonic darkness come from? Oh, from the greatest act in history—from the completed work of the cross of Christ Jesus our Lord and by agreeing with the words of Jesus on the cross, "It is finished!"

Now let's go forth testifying (see Rev. 12:11) what the blood of Jesus has accomplished for us! Get ready; take aim; now fire!

◆

REFLECTION QUESTIONS

1. What is the greatest act in all of history? Describe it, please.
2. How was the blood of Jesus shed? How many times?
3. What are the biblical benefits of the shed blood of Jesus? What does this mean for you?

RECOMMENDED READING

The Blood of the Cross by Andrew Murray (Whitaker House, 1981)
Power in the Blood by Charles Spurgeon (Whitaker House, 1996)
The Cross of Christ by Andrew Murray (Marshal Pickering, 1989)

ENDNOTES

1. Jim and Michal Ann Goll, *Encounters With a Supernatural God* (Shippensburg, PA: Destiny Image, 1998), 98.

2. Wesley Duewel, *Mighty Prevailing Power* (Grand Rapids, MI: Zondervan Publishing House, 1990), 308.

3. Charles Spurgeon, *Twelve Sermons on Prayer*, as quoted in Duewel, *Mighty Prevailing Prayer*, 308.

4. This quote comes from a personal testimony I have heard through my relationship with healing evangelist Mahesh Chavda, now residing in Charlotte, North Carolina, concerning a ministry trip of his into Zaire, Africa.

5. Lewis E. Jones, "There Is Power in the Blood." Public domain.

Chapter 11

SMART BOMBS OF PRAISE AND PRAYER

D uring the bombing raids of World War II, the airmen
had to drop up to nine thousand bombs to hit a specific target. These missions required a large number of flights, as
each plane deployed could carry only a small number of bombs.
Sad to say, this created a "high risk" factor endangering the lives
of thousands of airmen. Though attempting to hit a designated
target, the bombardiers were only assured they could direct a hit
within a quarter of a mile area.

In contrast, today's "smart bombs" can zero in on an object
three square feet in size from a long distance away. With today's
new laser-guided high-level technology, it takes only one bomb,
one plane, one pilot. The guidance systems are precise and the
hits often devasting to the enemy.

In correlation, the Lord wants to rearm His spiritual warriors with "smart bombs of praise and prayer" guided with pre-
cision, discernment, and wisdom to wreak havoc in the enemy's
territory. This is a day of increased knowledge, great teaching im-
partation, and godly veteran mentors who are qualified to lead
the global prayer and praise movement where it has never gone
before. Let's cultivate the right spiritual atmosphere through authentic "harp and bowl" engagements and thus dispel the powers
of darkness by releasing the brilliance of His great presence!

THE CENTRAL FOCUS AND ACTIVITY

Although the call of the Church is to make disciples, the central activity of the Church is prayer and worship. One of satan's
primary strategies is to distract the Church—to divert us from
our central focus. Prayer is the conduit through which both the

wisdom to know the will and ways of God and the power to do the work of God are imparted.

The great nineteenth-century English poet Tennyson once wrote, "More things are wrought by prayer than this world dreams of."[1] How right he was. Prayer is the key, the secret behind every advance of the Kingdom of God in the earth. Every great revival of the Church, every breakthrough of the gospel into new areas or people groups, every defeat of a demonic stronghold has been preceded by a protracted season of prayer from committed, ordinary believers.

One of the most exciting and significant characteristics of the current move of God is that He is restoring to the Church an understanding of prayer's centrality in everything we do. In our zeal to be about our Lord's work, we sometimes neglect prayer—shortchanging our ministry and effectiveness in the process. John Wesley once said, "God does everything by prayer, and nothing without it." In his dynamic book *The Hidden Power of Prayer and Fasting*, my dear friend Mahesh Chavda, who certainly has experience with both, writes,

> The Lord is opening our eyes to the simple truth that prayer is where everything begins and ends in the realm of the Spirit. It is here that everything is accomplished. Prayer is the true genetic code of the Church. We have received other mutant genes that have caused us to evolve away from God's true design for His Body. *Nothing that God is going to do will happen without prayer.*[2]

In readjusting the Church's focus on "smart bomb praying," the Lord is restoring old methods and revealing new applications, both individual and corporate. One of the significant characteristics of this is the practice of "praying with insight."

INSIGHT, DISCERNMENT, AND WISDOM

What does "praying with insight" mean? It means praying from the perspective of knowledge or understanding regarding the circumstances of the person or situation you are assigned to. Insight is the power to see below the surface of a situation, to discern the inner nature or truth of something that is not immediately apparent. Praying with insight combines being informed with knowledge and by prophetic revelation.

Similar to insight in source and meaning is discernment, the ability to comprehend that which is obscure, to distinguish or discriminate (in the positive sense) between good and evil, true and false, right and wrong, especially where (on the surface at least) the differences are very subtle. "And this I pray, that your love may abound still more and more in real knowledge and all discernment, so that you may approve the things that are excellent" (Phil. 1:9-10a).

Wisdom is a quality related to insight and discernment, and is the beginning of the fear of the Lord. It is the ability to discern inner qualities and relationships and to make practical application of experience, knowledge, and information. One of my prayers from childhood has been, "Give me wisdom beyond my years." I have prayed James 1:5 as much as any Scripture in the Bible, "But if any of you lacks wisdom, let him ask of God, who gives to all generously and without reproach, and it will be given to him."

Insight, discernment, wisdom—all are critical qualities for effective prayer. God gives insight because whenever He gets ready to move, He reveals His plans to those who are seeking Him. "Then you will see this, and your heart will be glad, and your bones will flourish like the new grass; and the hand of the Lord will be made known to His servants, but He will be indignant toward His enemies" (Is. 66:14); "Surely the Lord God does nothing unless He reveals His secret counsel to His servants the prophets" (Amos 3:7).

Praying with insight is a key strategy that the Lord is restoring to His Church in these days. But just as there are different types of military weapons, so there are many different forms of prayer in God's warchest, such as praying on-site, prayer-walking, prayer watches, prayer and fasting, reminding God of His Word, etc.

PRAYING ON-SITE

On-site prayer is a fresh application of an ancient practice that the Holy Spirit is reviving in our generation. Praying on-site is directed, purposeful intercession, typically for a preset period of time, conducted in the very places we expect our prayers to be answered. It is insightful prayer, with research and geographical identification combined with dependency on the Holy Spirit's guidance to determine the specific needs and issues. In other words, it is responsive, researched, and revealed insight.

Praying on-site is not an exercise for the spiritual "elite" (if there is such a thing); it is a movement among everyday believers. The styles and approaches are as unique and varied as the people involved, ranging from carefully planned strategies to spontaneous Spirit-given prompts; from lofty appeals to pinpointed petitions; from a sharp focus on family and neighborhood to broader intercession for an entire campus, city, or nation.

Everyday believers are praying house by house in their neighborhoods, spreading God's love by being lighthouses of prayer. Students are marching in quiet prayer through their high schools and college campuses. Consider, for example, the annual "See You at the Pole" rallies. What began with one youth group in Texas has grown to include thousands of Christian students on hundreds of public school campuses across the nation. Together they gather around their schools' flagpoles to pray for each other, for their fellow students, for their teachers and administrators, and for their schools.

On-site intercession is a refreshing, creative expression of prayer that should supplement but never replace regular prayer meetings. As refreshment, it carries several significant benefits:

1. It thaws the ice.
2. It helps us overcome fear.
3. It helps us identify with our surroundings.
4. It helps us get God's heart.
5. It helps us confess sin.
6. It helps us proclaim God's promises.
7. It helps us worship God.

PRAYER-WALKING

Very similar to praying on-site, prayer-walking is another fresh expression of intercession that is occurring more and more frequently within the Body of Christ. It may be as simple in scope as stepping out your front door and walking the streets of your neighborhood, praying for the people you meet as well as for those you can't see behind the closed doors of their homes. On the other hand, it might be a carefully planned campaign to cover an entire city by walking intercessors who lift up to God cries of repentance or the power of prophetic declarations as they walk.

On an even larger scale is the international March for Jesus movement, an annual event that emphasizes the power of praise in the streets. In recent years more than sixty thousand people took part in Europe in strategic praise and prayer. Beginning in London, England, they crossed to the Continent and walked hundreds of kilometers, ending up in Berlin, Germany. It was a great public demonstration and proclamation of praise to the Lord. In recent years in the capital of Brazil over two million Marchers for Jesus have assembled. The Reconciliation Walk mentioned in Chapter 6 is another great example of prayer-walking.

PRAYER WATCHES

A prayer watch is a sustained prayer vigil over an extended period of time. Keeping a "watch" for the Lord is a thoroughly biblical principle. "But as for me, I will watch expectantly for the Lord; I will wait for the God of my salvation. My God will hear me" (Mic. 7:7).

Part of keeping the watch of the Lord is learning to wait on the Lord. "Wait for the Lord; be strong and let your heart take courage; yes, wait for the Lord" (Ps. 27:14); "Wait for the Lord, and keep His way, and He will exalt you to inherit the land; when the wicked are cut off, you will see it" (Ps. 37:34). Now that's a powerful and encouraging promise for believers who want to reclaim the land from the enemy!

I believe the definitive example of a prayer watch would have to be that of the Moravians, whom I mentioned earlier. In the first chapter of my book *The Lost Art of Intercession*, I dealt with the Moravians at some length. Concerning their prayer watch I wrote:

> The Moravians over 100-year prayer vigil and global missionary exploits marked one of the purest moves of the Spirit in church history, and it radically changed the

expression of Christianity in their age. Many leaders today feel that virtually every great missionary endeavor of the eighteenth and nineteenth centuries—regardless of denominational affiliation—was in a very real sense part of the fruit of the Moravians' sacrificial service and prophetic intercessory prayer. Their influence continues to be felt even in our day.[3]

One of the best contemporary examples I know of a prayer watch is the "Watch of the Lord" established by Mahesh and Bonnie Chavda at All Nations Church in Charlotte, North Carolina. Mahesh describes how it came about:

The Watch of the Lord™ began in January of 1995 when the Lord said to us, "Watch with Me." In response we invited about 20 people to spend from 10:00 p.m. Friday until 6:00 a.m. Saturday keeping the "night watch," which is going without sleep for spiritual reasons.

We waited on God in worship and prayer, and shared in communion through Jesus' body and blood represented in the Lord's Supper. Every Friday since then, we have done the same. We have celebrated the watch with thousands of watchmen present. Watch groups have now sprung up throughout the United States and around the globe. We find ourselves in the midst of a renewed visitation that is manifesting the glory of the Lord![4]

I eat, live, and have my being in this arena of prayer. I have the joy of hosting various weekly "prayer watches" at our House of David in Tennessee. Want to join Mahesh, myself, and others in sacrificing some time for spiritual purposes? Then "watch and pray" with me for a while!

PRAYER AND FASTING

Fasting is another powerful prayer practice that is seeing a great revival in these days. Except for scattered brief periods of time or extraordinary individuals, for much of the history of the Church fasting has been tucked away in the closet of the outdated fashions of spiritual clothing. In recent years, however, more and more people have begun to take it out of mothballs, smooth it out, and dust it off. Many of these bold souls are discovering that fasting combined with prayer is a powerhouse punch, able to deliver a solid one-two knockout blow to the enemy. It also opens the channel for a greater outpouring of the glory, power, and presence of God.

Fasting is the discipline of going without food for certain specified periods of time for spiritual reasons. The length and type of fast will vary according to the individual and the situation.

Why should we fast, anyway? Mahesh Chavda in his book *The Hidden Power of Prayer and Fasting* gives nine reasons:[5]

1. We fast in obedience to God's Word.
2. We fast to humble ourselves before God and to obtain His grace and power.
3. We fast to overcome temptations in areas that keep us from moving into God's power.
4. We fast to be purified from sin (and to help others become purified as well).
5. We fast to become weak before God so God's power can be strong.
6. We fast to obtain God's support in order to accomplish His will.
7. We fast in times of crisis.
8. We fast when seeking God's direction.
9. We fast for understanding and divine revelation.

Beyond the reasons for fasting are the benefits of fasting. Mahesh lists seven.[6] He says that when we fast,

1. We humble ourselves.
2. We see life's priorities more clearly.
3. We see balance return to areas of our lives where there is imbalance.
4. Our selfish ambition and pride begin to be washed away.
5. We become more sensitive to God's Spirit, and the nine gifts of the Holy Spirit work more effectively in our lives.
6. Our hidden areas of weakness or susceptibility rise to the surface so that God can deal with them.
7. God makes us more unselfish.

Now let's see what damage we can do to the enemy's camp by investigating the power and passion of "bombs of praise."

BOMBS OF PRAISE: THE WEAPON OF DELIVERANCE

Have you ever wondered what God's "address" is? It is spelled p-r-a-i-s-e! It's quite simple. He inhabits the praises of His people. God resides in our praise! "Yet You are holy, O You who are enthroned upon the praises of Israel" (Ps. 22:3). God is holy and cannot dwell in an unholy place. Praise sanctifies the atmosphere. The Holy One is enthroned on the praises of His people. Whenever God seems far away, remember that He is really nearby. In fact, we could say that the Lord is as close as the praise on our lips! Now that's intimacy!

Since the very presence and power of God are "enthroned" on our praises, it is easy to see how praise is a very potent spiritual weapon. First of all, it is a means of deliverance. "He who sacrifices thank offerings honors Me, and he prepares the way so that I may show him the salvation of God" (Ps. 50:23 NIV). When we praise God in the midst of a terrible situation, salvation and deliverance enter in.

Praise is also a weapon that can silence the devil. "From the lips of children and infants You have ordained praise because of Your enemies, to silence the foe and the avenger" (Ps. 8:2 NIV). God has ordained praise that we might silence satan. If we carry the "high praises of God in our mouths" (see Ps. 149:6), satan will have no foothold in our lives and no basis from which to accuse us. Satan has no answer, no defense, against praise to God.

HIGH PRAISES: THE PLACE OF GOD'S DWELLING

Of course, our praise doesn't make God any bigger than He already is, though He seems bigger to us when we praise Him. Somehow praise ignites our faith and expands our vision and understanding of God. Perhaps this is because praise provides a habitation for God.

Praise shapes the attitude of our hearts. We can will ourselves to praise, even when we don't feel like it. Scripture simply commands us to praise. It doesn't matter whether we're having a good day or a bad day; whether we are sick or well; or whether or not we have all our tax returns ready for April 15. Praise is a choice. The Bible simply says, "Let everything that has breath praise the Lord. Praise the Lord!" (Ps. 150:6) Praise is contagious. Once we begin to praise the Lord with our mouths, it quickly spreads to our minds and our hearts.

Just as thanksgiving expresses gratitude to God for what He does, so praise acknowledges God for who He is. If worship relates to God's holiness and thanksgiving to God's goodness, then praise relates to God's greatness. "Great is the Lord, and greatly to be praised, in the city of our God, His holy mountain" (Ps. 48:1); "Great is the Lord, and highly to be praised; and His greatness is unsearchable" (Ps. 145:3).

No matter where we are, no matter how many or how few of us there are, whenever we praise the Lord we build a throne where He can come and sit among us in His manifested presence and speak to us in authority and intimacy. When we enthrone Christ in His glory on our praises, He can release His authority and power to us; and we can move out in strength and confidence to accomplish His will.

A Key to Impacting a City

Want to impact your city? Then realize, the entrance into the city of God is through the gate of praise (see Ps. 100:4). Speaking prophetically of Jerusalem, Isaiah says, "But you will call your walls salvation, and your gates praise" (Is. 60:18b). Jesus entered His city, the holy city, to the praises of the people. They threw down their garments and cast palm branches across His way as they shouted, "Blessed is He who comes in the name of the Lord!" (Mt. 21:9b)

It was praise that welcomed and ushered Jesus into the last week of His earthly ministry, and it will be praise that ushers Him into His end-time ministry in the earth through His Body, the Church. Once again praise will pave the way and build a highway for our God. Then the Lord will descend from Heaven with a roar of triumph and usher in His eternal reign.

I believe that one of the best things the church in a city could do today in this regard is to go on a prolonged fast of not criticizing any other parts of Christ's Body. It would take enormous power away from the enemy if we would pledge ourselves not to compete, compare, speak against, or slander any other churches or denominations, but speak only blessings, encouragement, and edification. This would derail one of satan's primary strategies and stop him dead in his tracks. It would revolutionize the Church and transform the world!

Yes, practical applications of prayer and praise are proceeding forth in various cities where united prayer of the "watchmen on the walls" is being submitted to the "gatekeepers of cities" (pastoral and apostolic leaders). Today, in Nashville, Tennessee, I have the privilege of walking with other "city intercessors" who gather once a month to cry out to the Lord on behalf of Music City U.S.A. to be changed into "Worship City to the World." Yes, it is time for the "gatekeepers and watchmen" to bring an impact to our cities together.

THE BALANCE BEAM

Praise and worship maintains our center of balance in the exercise of spiritual warfare. Jack Hayford once said, "Worship is the most important key to maintaining a balanced life. I've never seen a worshiper become unbalanced." A proper understanding of the role of worship will help keep us balanced in our expression of spiritual warfare.

The best place to look for a picture of balance for warfare is the cross. The cross was the ultimate battle. In triumph Christ thundered out, "It is finished!" and forever sealed the devil's fate. Yes, our agreeing, worshiping, praising, and thanking the Father for the work of the cross of Christ is a balance beam that we must walk upon.

So when it comes to maintaining our equilibrium in spiritual warfare, the plumb has to fall where the greatest battle has been fought and won, and that's the cross. What keeps us with our face pointed toward the cross? Praise, prayer, worship and intercession!

The Victory Is Ours!

As a spiritual weapon, praise is the way to release Christ's victory. Let us praise the Lord by any and all means available to us. The "high praises of God in our mouths" release His power to the maximum in our lives and our churches. There is something irreplaceable about learning to praise God for ourselves. Praise is one of the highest expressions of spiritual warfare. It can place demonic principalities in chains (see Ps. 149:6-9). In praise, we simply declare that which is already written in the Word of God: "It is finished."

The outcome of the great war between Christ and satan, between good and evil, has already been decided at the cross. By the death and resurrection of Jesus Christ, God disarmed all the satanic forces. With our praise we enforce and extend the victory Christ has already won at Calvary. This is an honor given to all His holy ones! Because victory is His, victory is now ours! Praise the Lord!

REFLECTION QUESTIONS

1. What does it mean to pray with insight?
2. What is "prayer-walking," and what is its value?
3. What are some of the biblical benefits of offering up the high praises of God?

RECOMMENDED READING

Prayer-Walking by Steve Hathorne and Graham Kendrick (Creation House, 1993)

The Hidden Power of Prayer and Fasting by Mahesh Chavada (Destiny Image Publishers, 1998)

Worship: The Pattern of Things in Heaven by Joseph Garlington (Destiny Image, 1997)

ENDNOTES

1. Quoted in John Bartlett, *Bartlett's Familiar Quotations, 16th ed.*, Justin Kaplan, ed. (New York: Little, Brown and Company, 1992), 459:27.

2. Mahesh Chavda, *The Hidden Power of Prayer and Fasting* (Shippensburg, PA: Destiny Image Publishers, 1998), 132. Emphasis in the original.

3. Jim W. Goll, *The Lost Art of Intercession* (Shippensburg, PA: Revival Press, 1997), 4.

4. Chavda, *The Hidden Power of Prayer and Fasting*, 148, note 2.

5. Chavda, *The Hidden Power of Prayer and Fasting*, 37-49.

6. Chavda, *The Hidden Power of Prayer and Fasting*, 118-120.

Chapter 12

THE FINAL SHOT

◆

By this time many of you who have stayed with me so far may be asking, "Okay, Jim, what's next? What are you saving for the final shot? What are you saving for the knockout punch? What is the ammo you are waiting to load into our gospel guns to fire?"

Perhaps the Spirit of God has stirred up in you through these pages an awareness of the crying need for corporate confession and representational repentance for the lifting of generational sins and curses from our lives, land, and the nations. Perhaps you are reaching deeper now into the heart of God ready to declare forth His promises and with them shatter the powers of darkness.

Even though we have faced many sobering and convicting truths in these pages, I want to assure you, that in Christ, you are on the winning side! I want to unveil for you one of the unique characteristics of our Father God's nature—our God is a mighty warrior.

BORN FOR BATTLE

As children of God we were born in the midst of a war and we were born for war. As children of God we are agents of light behind enemy lines in a world trapped in darkness. We cannot avoid the conflict. The issue is not whether we battle, but how we battle. As far as I am concerned, effective intercession includes being a "battle axe for Jesus!"

From the beginning of time, the satanic powers of darkness have fought savagely against God and against everything He stands for. Now, realize that all true spiritual warfare centers around the placement of the Son of God. The collision of Heaven and earth is the battlefield; at stake is the eternal spiritual destiny of humanity. It is a conflict of cosmic proportions; it is an all-out war to the death, winner-take-all with no quarter given to the loser.

Each of us who has been born again by the Spirit of God through the death and resurrection of Jesus Christ was born into a Kingdom that is geared for war. As citizens of that Kingdom and as members of the royal family we have been groomed for battle since day one. Our Father, the King, has provided every re-source we need—training, clothing, and weapons—and expects us to take to the field to fight in His name, under His authority, and with His power. Victory is assured; the enemy, in fact, has al-ready been defeated. Christ won the victory on the cross. The day is coming when Christ will return in glory and all His enemies will be put under His feet (see Mt. 16:27; 22:44). Until that day, however, the war rages on, and we are called to do our part.

When the Messiah came He crushed the serpent's head, de-stroying satan's right to rule over us. By His death and resurrec-tion Christ crushed satan's nerve center—his strategies and power. Remember what happens when you crush or cut off the head of a snake? The body thrashes about wildly for a little bit. When Christ crushed the serpent's head, satan, realizing that his time was short, went on a wild fling, thrashing violently about trying to bite, spill blood, and spread venom wherever, however, and to whomever he could.

Although satan's power and authority over us have been de-stroyed, his final destruction lies in the future. "The God of peace will soon crush Satan under your feet" (Rom. 16:20a). The com-ing day of the final crushing of satan is described in the Book of Revelation: "And the devil who deceived them was thrown into the lake of fire and brimstone, where the beast and the false prophet are also; and they will be tormented day and night for-ever and ever" (Rev. 20:10).

OUR LORD IS A MAN OF WAR

According to Exodus 15:3, the Lord is a warrior; Romans 16:20 says he is "the God of peace." He is both. Peace comes through war. On the world stage, treaties result from the resolution of conflicts, and the parties involved have the responsibility of observing and enforcing the terms of the treaty. In the spiritual realm, Christ overcame and defeated satan and established victory for the Kingdom of Heaven. The enforcement of Christ's victory in the earth is enacted through us as we follow in obedience and walk in the character of Christ. This is one of the reasons that I believe we have a part to play in determining how long satan's "final fling" lasts. At any rate, we are soldiers in God's army and are called to the fray. The God of peace will crush satan under our feet, and the only place where that can happen is on the field of battle.

If we as children of God are born in the midst of a great war and are called to war, then there must be a part of our Father's nature and character in which He Himself is a warrior. The Scriptures support this view of God. When Moses was preparing Joshua to lead the nation of Israel into the Promised Land, he said to Joshua concerning the nations they would meet across the Jordan River, "Do not fear them, for the Lord your God is the one fighting for you" (Deut. 3:22). When Isaiah prophesied judgment against Babylon, he spoke of "a sound of tumult on the mountains, like that of many people! A sound of the uproar of kingdoms, of nations gathered together! The Lord of hosts is mustering the army for battle" (Is. 13:4).

Our Lord is a warrior, and He is mustering His army for battle against the forces of darkness. We need not fear marching under His banner because He will not be defeated. "But thanks be to God, who always leads us in triumph in Christ" (2 Cor. 2:14a). The key here is following where God leads. Wherever God leads, if we follow, we experience triumph.

Part of developing strategy is understanding the nature of the conflict. All-out war calls for all-out commitment from the warriors. Only through total allegiance to Christ and absolute surrender to His Lordship will we experience victory in spiritual warfare.

THE NATURE OF THE ENEMY

It is also important to understand the nature of the enemy. Paul wrote in Ephesians, "For our struggle is not against flesh and blood, but against the rulers, against the powers, against the world forces of this darkness, against the spiritual forces of wickedness in the heavenly places" (Eph. 6:12). Satan does not fight the way we do. We have been called for a wrestling match—for closed-in, hand-to-hand combat. Of all the "armor of God" that Paul describes in Ephesians 6:13-17—the belt of truth, the breast-plate of righteousness, the shoes of the gospel of peace, the shield of faith, the helmet of salvation, and the sword of the Spirit—all except the sword are primarily defensive in nature. They are de-signed to protect from attack near at hand. The sword is for at-tacking the enemy, but only when he is within arm's reach.

Satan, on the other hand, prefers to fight from a distance. Ephesians 6:16 says that we can use the shield of faith "to extin-guish all the flaming arrows of the evil one." Instead of coming in close, satan would rather shoot fiery arrows at us from the shadows. I believe that this is because he fears us. Satan knows that he is defeated and that we have an invincible ally. He knows he can't win, so he tries instead to produce in us an inordinate fear of him.

Now certainly we need to have a proper respect for satan's limited ability. He is still powerful—too powerful for any of us to take on in our own strength. However, it seems at times that satan understands the power available to us better than we do. He doesn't want us to get close enough to wrestle with him be-cause he knows that if we do, we just might lay hold of him and in the power of God knock him down for the count.

OVERPOWERING THE STRONG MAN

These strongholds can be broken. Once, when the Pharisees accused Jesus of casting out demons by demonic power, He re-sponded by saying that a house divided against itself would fall, then asked how satan's kingdom could stand if he was divided against himself (see Lk. 11:15-19). The absurdity of their argu-ment was plain. Then Jesus continued:

> But if I cast out demons by the finger of God, then the kingdom
> of God has come upon you. When a strong man, fully armed,
> guards his own house, his possessions are undisturbed. But

when someone stronger than he attacks him and overpowers him, he takes away from him all his armor on which he had relied and distributes his plunder (Luke 11:20-22).

C. Peter Wagner identifies the "strong man" as referring specifically to Beelzebub, a high-ranking demonic principality and probably a territorial spirit. The term can also apply to any demonic principality. The strong man's "possessions" are unsaved people whom he strives to keep in that condition. As long as the strong man is "fully armed," his "possessions" are "undisturbed."[1] If he is overpowered, however, his "possessions" can be set free. When the demonic authority is removed, those held in bondage by him can be released into the freedom of Christ.

Who, then, is the "someone stronger" who overpowers the strong man? Most people would immediately answer, "Jesus." Jesus is certainly stronger than any demonic principality, but C. Peter Wagner says that Jesus was not referring specifically to Himself, but rather to the Holy Spirit. The key to understanding this is in the phrase "the finger of God" in verse 20. In Matthew's parallel account, Jesus says, "But if I cast out demons by the Spirit of God..." (Mt. 12:28). "The 'finger of God' is therefore a synonym for the Holy Spirit."[2] It was through the power of the Holy Spirit that Jesus cast out demons.

WHERE DOES THAT LEAVE US?

How are we to see removed the demonic authority that binds our cities, our nations, and our world? How are we to tear down the walls of estrangement that centuries of generational sin have erected? We are to do it the same way Jesus did—in the power of the Holy Spirit. Again, here is C. Peter Wagner:

Only the Holy Spirit can overcome the territorial spirits, destroy their armor and release the captives under their wicked control. Where is the Holy Spirit today? He is in us who have been born again and have asked God to fill us with the Holy Spirit. Jesus' last words ever spoken directly to His disciples were, "But you shall receive power when the Holy Spirit has come upon you; and you shall be witnesses to Me" (Acts 1:8). Here we find spiritual power tied in directly with evangelism. Jesus assured His disciples that the same power He used while on earth would be fully available to them. And it was up to them to move out and do the work of evangelism."[3]

The same power that Jesus used is available to us! That is truly an awesome thought! The irresistible, probing "finger of God" can uproot and cast out all demonic powers and principalities, no matter how strong they are...and bring healing to the nations. That "finger" is in each of us as believers, and through the power of the Spirit we can see territorial demonic authority over our cities and nations removed. There is much to confess and forgive, and there is much restitution to be made.

The finger of God is at work in our world as never before, and I say, "Let it come!" I make this appeal, however: Let us pray that the finger of God will come first to us inwardly and bring cleansing. Then we can arise in the strength of the Lord and, "having done everything, to stand firm" (Eph. 6:13b) against the powers of darkness in the great name of Jesus! Just point out the sin, Lord, and we will wage war through personal and identificational repentance. We can remove the legal basis that allows the demonic forces of the air to remain by letting the finger of the Holy Spirit point into and pierce our hearts and remove the common ground we have held with the enemy—personally and generationally.

THE LEGAL BASIS OF DEMONIC ACTIVITY

As I mentioned in Chapter 2, the Lord gave me a word in New York in 1991 in which He said, "I will release new understandings of identification in intercession whereby the legal basis of the rights of the demonic powers of the air to remain will be removed." We need to take a brief look at the second part of that statement: the legal basis for demonic activity.

Conditions exist all over our world that give the demonic powers of the air "legal authority" to remain and operate against God's purpose and the good of humanity. I am convinced that a full global awakening cannot occur until this legal authority is removed. The only way to remove it is by the confession of the corporate and generational sins that established the authority in the first place, and their forgiveness through faith in Christ and the cleansing power of His blood. Then we turn and enforce the victory of Calvary through the power of proclamation, displacing darkness through praise warfare, and doing the works of Christ.

Demonic spirits have no true authority to influence an area without permission. Certain conditions give them access points, or authority, to set up a base of operations from whence they exercise their oppression. What are some of these conditions?

1. *Idolatry.*

Stated simply, idolatry is the worship of anything or anyone other than God. Our Lord is a jealous God, and He wants to eradicate and bring cleansing from anything that receives worship other than Him. You see, we become slaves to whomever or whatever we worship. Idols represent evil spirits (see 1 Cor. 10:19-20), and where idols exist, there also exists the legal right for the demonic spirits they represent to exercise influence.

2. *Temples to pagan religions.*

This deals not only with the construction of "high places" of demonic and occultic worship (see 2 Kings 17:11; Ps. 78:58; Jer. 19:5; 32:35), but also with more subtle, destructive forms such as Masonic lodges and other things of this nature that are of the luciferian foundation. Have mercy, dear God! Remove the high places in this generation.

3. *Murder and the shedding of innocent blood.*

"You shall not murder" (Ex. 20:13). "So you shall not pollute the land in which you are; for blood pollutes the land and no expiation can be made for the land for the blood that is shed on it, except by the blood of him who shed it" (Num. 35:33). Today, of course, we deal not only with external wars accompanied by great shedding of blood, but also with internal wars in the shedding of the blood of infants legally killed while hidden in the supposedly safe sanctuary of their mothers' wombs. "God have mercy," is all we can say!

4. *Witchcraft.*

"There shall not be found among you anyone who makes his son or his daughter pass through the fire, one who uses divination, one who practices witchcraft, or one who interprets omens, or a sorcerer, or one who casts a spell, or a medium, or a spiritist, or one who calls up the dead. For whoever does these things is detestable to the Lord" (Deut. 18:10-12a). In the United States all you have to do is turn on almost any television set and you can be exposed to witchcraft practitioners under the guise of giving you "your word for the day" and be blasted by satan's deception. "Deliver us," must be our cry!

5. *The removal of prayer and Bible reading from our schools.*

The beginning of the current moral and spiritual deterioration of American society coincides with the day prayer and Bible reading were declared unlawful in the United States' public education system. When God was "kicked out," the god of secular humanism filled the void. Whenever we assume God's position and take it upon ourselves to solve problems that only Deity can handle, we make ourselves out to be gods. This progressive deterioration of our society has been shockingly driven home by recent shootings and murders at our various public school institutions.

6. *Adultery, sodomy, perversion, and all other sexual sins.*

These all represent the twisting and distorting of a God-given drive in order to satisfy man's sinful desires and lustful imaginations. Historically, much idol worship has been linked with immoral and perverted sexual practices. (See Leviticus 18 and 20; Deuteronomy 23:17 and Romans 1:24-28.) This one category alone is enough to keep you weeping before God for the rest of the day. How we have fallen from our first love! This is not just the sin of the world; it is the sin of a modern-day, worldly Church! Forgive us!

7. *Substance abuse—alcohol, drugs, etc.*

This is nothing more than witchcraft under a deceptively "fun" disguise, and as such it gives entrance for demonic powers to have a legal basis to rule. Revelation 21:8 and 22:15 mention the word *sorcerers*, which in Greek is *pharmakeus*. It is derived from *pharmakon*, which means a drug or spell-giving potion. So the use of drugs is related to witchcraft, or the "magic arts." Let us repent of our acts of sorcery and witchcraft and close this legal access point of the devil's blatant schemes.

8. *Fighting, anger, hatred, cursing, and unforgiveness.*

These are all dangerous attitudes and mind-sets that can open the door for demonic activity. "He who returns evil for good, evil will not depart from his house" (Prov. 17:13). First Peter 3:9 says that we are not to return evil for evil or insult for insult, but to give a blessing instead. Tied in with all this is the importance of forgiveness (see Mt. 18:21-35), of having clean hearts as we approach the Lord's table (see 1 Cor. 11:27-30), and being in proper relationship with those in authority (see Ex. 20:12; Rom. 13:1-2).

These are just eight categories that give the enemy a legal basis of operation. I'm sure there are more. But don't get depressed now; look up! There is a promise for every problem.

RISING TO THE CHALLENGE

In his book *Warfare Prayer*, C. Peter Wagner writes,

Suppose demonic strongholds actually exist in a nation or a city, affecting society in general and resistance to the gospel in particular. What can be done about it?

Just as in the case of demonized individuals, if sin is present, repentance is called for, if curses are in effect they need to be broken, and if emotional scars are causing pain, inner healing is needed. We know from the Old Testament that nations can be guilty of corporate sins. This was not only true of Gentile nations, but of Israel as well. Both Nehemiah and Daniel give us examples of godly persons who felt the burden for sins of their nations.

It is important to note that both Nehemiah and Daniel, while they were standing before God on behalf of their entire nation, confessed not only the corporate sins of their people, but also their individual sins. Those who remit the sins of nations must not fail to identify personally with the sins that were or are being committed even though they might not personally be as guilty of them as some other sins.[3]

God is looking for people who are ready and willing to stand in the gap for their families, cities, and nations. He is searching for people who, through targeted intercession, will take on the burdens of corporate and generational sin and not simply carry them and be weighed down, but carry them away like the scapegoat in the wilderness. Then, it is my conviction, that the legal basis for the powers of the air to remain will be removed and the blessing, healing, and restoration of the Lord can potentially come down.

Will you rise to the challenge? Will you enter into that place of identification and confession and cry out to God with me? Then let's turn and proclaim that "greater is He who is with us than He who is in the world."

IF WE WILL, HE WILL

If we will do what God has told us to do—intercede—then He will do what He said He would do—cleanse and heal us.

If My people, which are called by My name, shall humble themselves, and pray, and seek My face, and turn from their wicked ways; then will I hear from heaven, and will forgive their sin, and will heal their land (2 Chronicles 7:14 KJV).

I am willing to go on this journey to hold back darkness and call forth the light of our Father's mercy. Are you? But wait—I have a promise for you. Do you know what promise follows the prayer, "Father, forgive us!"? It is, "Do not lead us into temptation, but deliver us from evil" (Mt. 6:13a). Guess what?

Deliverance follows confession!
Resurrection from the dead will occur!
Life will spring forth!
If we will, He will!

Our greatest destiny in the Church and our nations could be right in front of our eyes. For when we cry, "Papa, forgive us!" He comes running to our aid. So don't be in dismay—just cry out to the Lord!

Effective intercession embraces both sides of God's nature—it wars through confession and it enforces the victory through the passionate power of proclamation. Let history-shaping intercession arise across the globe in order that Jesus Christ may receive the rewards for His suffering!

With a passion for intercession,
Jim (James) W. Goll

REFLECTION QUESTIONS

1. Recite three scriptures describing God as a man of war.
2. What are some of the legal bases for demonic activity?
3. Effective intercession involves the bringing together of two opposites—what are they?

RECOMMENDED READING

Engaging the Enemy by C. Peter Wagner (Regal Books, 1991)
Ridding Your Home of Spiritual Darkness by Chuck Pierce and Rebecca Wagner Systema (Wagner Leadership Institute, 1999)

ENDNOTES

1. C. Peter Wagner, *Confronting the Powers: How the New Testament Church Experienced the Power of Strategic-Level Spiritual Warfare* (Ventura, CA: Regal Books, 1996), 149-150.

2. C. Peter Wagner, *Confronting the Powers*, 149-150.

3. C. Peter Wagner, *Confronting the Powers*, 149.

4. C. Peter Wagner, *Warfare Prayer* (Ventura, CA: Regal Books, 1992), 130-131.

Jim and Michal Ann Goll

A CALL TO THE SECRET PLACE
by Michal Ann Goll

Deep inside each one of us is a longing to escape the frantic pace of life in the 21st Century. *A Call to the Secret Place* is your personal invitation to take that step towards the place lovingly prepared for you. Cheering you on will be the voices of other women as shared by Michal Ann Goll—women on the frontlines like Madam Guyon, Susanna Wesley, Fanny Crosby, Basilea Schlink, Gwen Shaw, Beth Alves, and others. Their collective voices call out inviting you to join them in the privacy of a loving moment with your Lord.

ISBN 0-7684-2179-9

ELIJAH'S REVOLUTION
by Jim W. Goll and Lou Engle

A holy revolution of unprecedented dimension is underway today in America. In the face of relentless spiritual and moral decay, thousands of believers are answering God's call to a holy life of total and radical abandonment to Christ. Fired with the bold spirit of Elijah and the self giving heart of Esther, these latter day revolutionaries seek nothing less than the complete transformation of society through revival and spiritual awakening.

ISBN 0-7684-2057-1

WASTED ON JESUS
by Jim Goll

Wasted on Jesus defines a new generation of passionate lovers of the Lord Jesus. within the pages of this book you will be introduced to the hunger and passion of these 'wasted ones.' You will experience the collision of religion with reality, theology with thirst, and legalism with extravagant love.

ISBN 0-7684-2103-9

THE LOST ART OF INTERCESSION
by Jim Goll

When God's people send 'up' the incense of prayer and worship, God will send 'down' supernatural power, anointing, and acts of intervention. Jim Goll paints a picture of prophetic clarity and urgency in this anointed work that sounds God's clarion call to His Church: This is the season for us to mount the walls with prayer and praise and restore *The Lost Art of Intercession*!

ISBN 1-56043-697-2

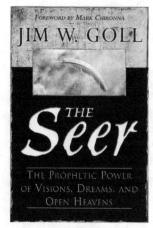

THE SEER

*The Prophetic Power of Visions,
Dreams, and Open Heavens*

Jim W. Goll

The prophetic movement in the church is fed by two mighty streams: the prophet, whose revelation is primarily verbal, and the seer, whose revelation is more visionary in nature. While the role of the prophet is familiar, little is known about the seer. Join author Jim W. Goll on an exciting and insightful journey into this lesser-known dimension-the visionary world of the seer. How does visionary revelation happen? Can any believer become a seer, or is this a prophetic dimension reserved for the specially gifted? *The Seer* will move your heart and stir up your hunger for intimacy with God, "because the seer's goal is to reveal the man Christ Jesus!"

ISBN 0-7684-2232-9

WOMEN ON THE FRONT LINES

by Michal Ann Goll

History is filled with ordinary women who have changed the course of their generation. Here, Michal Ann Goll, co-founder of Ministry to the Nations with her husband Jim, shares how her own life was transformed and highlights nine women whose lives will impact yours! Every generation faces the same choices and issues; learn how you, too, can heed the call to courage and impact a generation.

ISBN 0-7684-2020-2

Available at your local Christian bookstore.

For more information and sample chapters, visit www.destinyimage.com

Additional copies of this book and other
book titles from DESTINY IMAGE are
available at your local bookstore.

For a complete list of our titles,
visit us at www.destinyimage.com
Send a request for a catalog to:

Destiny Image® Publishers, Inc.
P.O. Box 310
Shippensburg, PA 17257-0310

*"Speaking to the Purposes of God for This
Generation and for the Generations to Come"*